First World War
and Army of Occupation
War Diary
France, Belgium and Germany

58 DIVISION
174 Infantry Brigade
198 Machine Gun Company
7 December 1916 - 28 February 1918

WO95/3006/4

The Naval & Military Press Ltd
www.nmarchive.com
Published in association with The National Archives

Published by

The Naval & Military Press Ltd

Unit 10 Ridgewood Industrial Park,

Uckfield, East Sussex,

TN22 5QE England

Tel: +44 (0) 1825 749494

www.naval-military-press.com

www.nmarchive.com

This diary has been reprinted in facsimile from the original. Any imperfections are inevitably reproduced and the quality may fall short of modern type and cartographic standards.

© **Crown Copyright**
Images reproduced by permission of The National Archives, London, England, 2015.

Contents

Document type	Place/Title	Date From	Date To
Heading	WO95/3006/4		
Heading	198th Machine Gun Coy Mar 1917-Feb 1918		
Heading	War Diary Volume IV March 1917 198 Company M.G.C		
War Diary	Bailleulmont	01/03/1917	22/03/1917
War Diary	Pommier	23/03/1917	25/03/1917
War Diary	Hamelincourt	26/03/1917	27/03/1917
War Diary	Pommier	28/03/1917	29/03/1917
War Diary	Bout-Des-Pres	30/03/1917	31/03/1917
Heading	War Diary 198 Machine Gun Company Volume V April 1917		
War Diary	Bout Des Pres	01/04/1917	01/04/1917
War Diary	Ligny	02/04/1917	02/04/1917
War Diary	Fontaine L'Etalon	03/04/1917	04/04/1917
War Diary	Mailly-Maillet	05/04/1917	07/04/1917
War Diary	Mailly	08/04/1917	12/04/1917
War Diary	Bihucourt	13/04/1917	30/04/1917
Heading	War Diary of 198th Machine Gun Company For The Month Of May 1917 Volume VI		
War Diary	Bihucourt	01/05/1917	07/05/1917
War Diary	In The Field	08/05/1917	14/05/1917
War Diary	Bihucourt	15/05/1917	15/05/1917
War Diary	Sapignies	16/05/1917	16/05/1917
War Diary	Mort Homme	17/05/1917	31/05/1917
Heading	198th Machine Gun Company War Diary Volume VII June 1917		
War Diary	Mort Homme	01/06/1917	04/06/1917
War Diary	Mory	05/06/1917	17/06/1917
War Diary	Vraucourt-St Leger Road (B.4.d)	18/06/1917	18/06/1917
War Diary	B.4.d	19/06/1917	24/06/1917
War Diary	Mory	25/06/1917	26/06/1917
War Diary	Courcelles	27/06/1917	30/06/1917
Heading	War Diary of 198 M.G. Coy 1/7/17 To 31/7/17 Vol 8		
War Diary	Courcelles	01/07/1917	06/07/1917
War Diary	Bancourt	07/07/1917	07/07/1917
War Diary	Fins	08/07/1917	10/07/1917
War Diary	Metz	11/07/1917	14/07/1917
War Diary	Metz En Couture	15/07/1917	16/07/1917
War Diary	Metz	17/07/1917	30/07/1917
War Diary	Neuville	31/07/1917	31/07/1917
War Diary	Simencourt	01/08/1917	24/08/1917
War Diary	Poperinghe	25/08/1917	28/08/1917
War Diary	Reigersberg	29/08/1917	29/08/1917
War Diary	Canal Bank	30/08/1917	30/08/1917
War Diary	Yser Canal Bank	31/08/1917	31/08/1917
Heading	198 Machine Gun Company M.G.C War Diary Volume X		
War Diary	Yser Canal Bank	01/09/1917	02/09/1917
War Diary	Canal Bank	03/09/1917	12/09/1917
War Diary	Dambre	13/09/1917	19/09/1917

War Diary	Alberta	20/09/1917	21/09/1917
War Diary	Reigersburg	22/09/1917	30/09/1917
Heading	198th Coy M.G.C War Diary A.F.C 2118 Volume XI October 1917		
War Diary	Reigersberg Camp	01/10/1917	01/10/1917
War Diary	Clerques	02/10/1917	20/10/1917
War Diary	Poperinghe	21/10/1917	24/10/1917
War Diary	Seige Camp	25/10/1917	27/10/1917
War Diary	In The Line At Poelcappelle	28/10/1917	31/10/1917
Heading	War Diary of 198th Company Machine Gun Corps From November 1st 1917 To December 1st 1917 Volume X		
War Diary	Siege Camp	01/11/1917	09/11/1917
War Diary	Kempton Park	10/11/1917	11/11/1917
War Diary	In The Line Poelcappelle	12/11/1917	16/11/1917
War Diary	Siege Camp	17/11/1917	17/11/1917
War Diary	Herzeele	18/11/1917	24/11/1917
War Diary	Proven	25/11/1917	25/11/1917
War Diary	Affringues	26/11/1917	26/11/1917
War Diary	Watterdal	27/11/1917	30/11/1917
Operation(al) Order(s)	198 Machine Gun Company Order No II	24/11/1917	24/11/1917
Heading	War Diary of 198th Company Machine Gun Corps From December 1st 1917 To January 1st 1918 Volume XIII (Original)		
War Diary	Watterdal	01/12/1917	06/12/1917
War Diary	Affringues	07/12/1916	07/12/1916
War Diary	Brown Camp on Poperinghe Elverdinghe Road	08/12/1917	08/12/1917
War Diary	Brown Camp	09/12/1917	10/12/1917
War Diary	Kempton Park	11/12/1917	20/12/1917
War Diary	Canal Bank	21/12/1917	21/12/1917
War Diary	Solferino Camp	22/12/1917	28/12/1917
War Diary	Kempton Park	29/12/1917	31/12/1917
Operation(al) Order(s)	198 Machine Gun Company Move Order No.4	06/12/1917	06/12/1917
Operation(al) Order(s)	Relief Orders No.1 By Lieut C.S Gamon For O.C 198 M.G Coy	11/12/1917	11/12/1917
Miscellaneous	Relief Orders Of 198 M.G Company No. 5	19/12/1917	19/12/1917
Heading	War Diary of 198th Company Machine Gun Corps From January 1st 1918 To February 1st 1918 Volume XIV (Original)		
War Diary	Kempton Park	01/01/1918	04/01/1918
War Diary	Solferino Camp	05/01/1918	07/01/1918
War Diary	Tunnelling Camp	08/01/1918	08/01/1918
War Diary	Road Camp	09/01/1918	20/01/1918
War Diary	Courcelles	21/01/1918	31/01/1918
Miscellaneous	198th Coy M.G.C Appendix I		
Miscellaneous	198 Machine Gun Company More Order	17/01/1918	17/01/1918
Heading	198th Machine Gun Coy War Diary Volume XV Feb 1918		
War Diary	Courcelles	01/02/1918	07/02/1918
War Diary	Roye	08/02/1918	08/02/1918
War Diary	Courcelles	08/02/1918	08/02/1918
War Diary	Crissolles	09/02/1918	09/02/1918
War Diary	Marizeele	10/02/1918	28/02/1918

WO 95/3006/4

198TH MACHINE GUN COY.
MAR 1917 – FEB 1918

From 12 Div

Should be part of 3006

Vol 4
12

Crown from 129

WAR DAIRY.
VOLUME IV
~~FEB~~ MARCH 1917

198 Company M.G.C.

WAR DIARY
or
INTELLIGENCE SUMMARY
(Erase heading not required.)

Army Form C. 2118.

Instructions regarding War Diaries and Intelligence Summaries are contained in F. S. Regs., Part II. and the Staff Manual respectively. Title Pages will be prepared in manuscript.

Place	Date 1917	Hour	Summary of Events and Information	Remarks and references to Appendices
BAILLEULMONT	MARCH 1		GASTINEAU was blown up by R.E. The enemy used this house to register on with their artillery. Enemy M.G's swept RIDGE ROAD at intervals during the night. Indirect fire was carried out on RANSART – ADINFER Road from 7 to 9 P.M. also in RANSART – BLAIREVILLE Road from 7. to 9. P.M. 3000 Rounds fired. WORK done. New emplacement at No 10 gun. Repairing trench at No 11 gun. General Situation NORMAL. WIND N.W.	R.J.M Capt
"	2		Enemy T.M's shelled our front line rather heavily in the afternoon commencing about 3 P.M. Enemy M.G's again swept RIDGE ROAD at night. WORK DONE. New entrance to Section A & commenced at GASTINEAU. Emplacements built up in support line. Indirect fire carried out on RANSART – ADINFER Road from 6. to 9.30 P.M. Situation NORMAL except rather heavy T.M activity in afternoon. WIND N.N.W.	R.J.M Capt

Army Form C. 2118.

WAR DIARY
INTELLIGENCE SUMMARY
(Erase heading not required.)

Instructions regarding War Diaries and Intelligence Summaries are contained in F. S. Regs., Part II. and the Staff Manual respectively. Title Pages will be prepared in manuscript.

Place	Date	Hour	Summary of Events and Information	Remarks and references to Appendices
BAIRLEULMONT	MAR 3		Enemy again shelled our front line & destroyed a M.G. emplacement at No 4 gun. Also demolished the end of LINCOLN LANE. Several shells fell near No 11 gun dug out during morning. Principally 5.9" shells. Hidinct fire carried out on RANSART-ADINFER Road from 6 to 10 P.M. – 1500 Rounds fired. Gas alarm was sounded on our left at 10 P.M. but was not taken up. General Situation – enemy artillery & M.M. active. RMW Capt. WIND.	
	4		During the night & early morning enemy T.M. blew in No 4 gun emplacement – gun was removed into the trench & no other damage occurred to gun or team. Enemy shelled Ridge Road by day & swept it with M.G. at night. Indirect fuel carried out on Road 73.a.4.1. & y13.a.6.7 & short bursts were fired from 6.30 to 10 P.M. Situation otherwise NORMAL. WIND. N.E – much colder. RMW Capt.	

249 Wt. W14957/M90 750,000 1/16 J.B.C. & A. Forms/C.2118/12.

WAR DIARY
INTELLIGENCE SUMMARY
(Erase heading not required.)

Army Form C. 2118.

Place	Date	Hour	Summary of Events and Information	Remarks and references to Appendices
BAILLEULMONT	1917 MAR 6		Enemy T.Ms were very active terminating in an intense barrage at 13 A.M. Under cover of this an enemy raiding party entered our trenches. They entered on the left of N°7 Gun (LIMERICK LANE) and passed along the trench towards the gun to alarm was given. The first the 2 sentries on the gun knew was that 2 infantry men ran towards them down the trench followed by about 10 Germans. A bomb was thrown wounding the 2 sentries slightly. The team in a dug out near were roused and came up the steps with more bombs. The Germans threw another bomb which killed Pte PTALUNA at the entrance to the dugout & lightly wounded 2/c SMITH (N°I Section). This MCB emptied their Revolvers into the Germans. The enemy then disappeared along the trench. The three men wounded were detained at Field Amb¹. 2/c SMITH A.S. PTE S. ROKLE W. and SAUNDERS S.W.A. Situation - after this situation was gain to NORMAL. Wind Nil - a light fall of snow.	RMM Capt

Army Form C. 2118.

WAR DIARY
or
INTELLIGENCE SUMMARY
(Erase heading not required.)

Instructions regarding War Diaries and Intelligence Summaries are contained in F. S. Regs., Part II. and the Staff Manual respectively. Title Pages will be prepared in manuscript.

Place	Date	Hour	Summary of Events and Information	Remarks and references to Appendices
BAILLEULMONT	MAR 6		WORK done. New emplacement at L'ALLOUETTE. No 7 gun was removed from front line and placed in a temporary position as in support line. Indirect fire carried out on RANSART – ADINFER Road (X 14 B 11.3 to X 14 B 9.5). General Situation Quiet. Full – N.E. Wind – fresh.	R.M. Capt.
"	7		3 shells fell in BELLACOURT village last night about 9 pm. As damage was slight no damage was slight S.O.S. again sealed front line in front of right sector. M.G. fire was shot to but head angle was nothing. Indirect fire carried out on following :— Old [illegible] Aream (X 3D 5.7 to X 14 A 3.8) 750 Rounds 6.30 pm to 8.30 pm. EXCELLEZEN WEG. 500 — 6.30 – 8.30 — RANSART – MONCHY Road. 1000 — 8 P.M. to 9 P.M. Full – N.E. Wind fresh.	R.M. Capt.

WAR DIARY
or
INTELLIGENCE SUMMARY

(Erase heading not required.)

Army Form C. 2118.

Place	Date	Hour	Summary of Events and Information	Remarks and references to Appendices
BAILLEULMONT	1917 MAR 8		Work done. Constructing shelters for gun teams. Targets engaged:- Ppied X.13.c. 2000 Rounds 5-6 P.M. 5 to 6 A.M. Ransart Adinfer Road 1000 — 9.0 A.M. to 11.30 A.M. RDM Capt. Situation. Quiet.	
"	9		Work done. Improving field of fire of No 2 a. Lt. position Targets engaged:- RANSART-ADINFER Road. 2000 Rds. 6 p.m. to 10.30 p.m. RDM Capt. Wind N.E. Situation Quiet. Work done Constructing Indirect fire positions at 1 and 3 guns.	
"	10		Targets engaged:- RANSART ADINFER Road 1000 Rds 6 P.M. to 10. P.M. Trench from X13 D 04 to X13 D 52 1000 Rds 6 P.M. to 10.30 P.M. RDM Capt. Situation Normal Wind S.W.	

Army Form C. 2118.

WAR DIARY
or
INTELLIGENCE SUMMARY

(Erase heading not required.)

Instructions regarding War Diaries and Intelligence Summaries are contained in F. S. Regs., Part II. and the Staff Manual respectively. Title Pages will be prepared in manuscript.

Place	Date	Hour	Summary of Events and Information	Remarks and references to Appendices
BAILLEUL-MENT	1917 MAR 11		Repairing and draining Section H.Q at GASTINEAU. A few gas shells fell during evening round BELLA COURT. Wind N.E. Situation Normal. RDM Capt.	
"	12		Constructing an extra emplacement for No 1 gun. Wind N.E. Situation quiet. RDM Capt.	
"	13		Constructing a position for barrage gun in LANARK work. Enemy T.M's active towards BERLES. Wind - mild - N.E. Situation Normal.	
"	14		Reps Commander visited the trenches in morning summoning at PARK ST at 11 A.M. A district fire position was constructed about 100 m. rear of front line - near LIMERICK LANE. Trees on RAMSART - MONCHY road were engaged. An enemy O.P. was suspected in these trees. Gun fired from 10 A.M till 12 noon. A man was observed behind the ridge evidently by looking for gun position. H.E and tear gas shells fell round V GASTINEAU about 6 P.M. Wind N.E. Situation Normal. RDM Capt.	

Army Form C. 2118.

WAR DIARY
— or —
INTELLIGENCE SUMMARY
(Erase heading not required.)

Instructions regarding War Diaries and Intelligence Summaries are contained in F. S. Regs., Part II. and the Staff Manual respectively. Title Pages will be prepared in manuscript.

Place	Date	Hour	Summary of Events and Information	Remarks and references to Appendices
BAILLEULMENT	1917 MAR 15.		6 guns were laid and ready to engage 2 roads and 4 C.T's in MONCHY from 5.15 A.M to 5.45 A.M to enfilade an attack, which 4 6" Divn'n attacked in the South. All these operations were cancelled. Took over whole of Bde front from BELLACOURT to BEARLES. 4 guns in front line near BEARLES. Wind W.E. RANGAFT — MONCHY Road. 1000 Rds. 8 P.M to 11.30 P.M RPM Capt Situation Normal.	
" "	16		Signs were observed of enemy preparing to retire. Fragment fires were observed in his reserve lines. Explosions were heard in his front line. Army Commander visited the trenches. He inspected the RENFREW and GASTINEAU gun positions. No fire was carried out today. Wind: W.L. Situation NORMAL. RPM Capt.	

WAR DIARY
INTELLIGENCE SUMMARY

Army Form C. 2118.

Place	Date	Hour	Summary of Events and Information	Remarks and references to Appendices
BAILEULMENT	1917 MAR 17		The Bde Major and Inspected the gun in the RAVINE. Noticed people being to this gun people are badly injured. Today everything was quiet. No rifle fire — no artillery. 8 P.M. fired on part of the enemy. We returned who held may in the open. We both were felt convinced the enemy had retired. About 4.30 P.M. it was reported that MONCHY had been evacuated by enemy. All guns had orders not to fire at all. Retreat in extraordinary quiet. RM Capt.	
	18		Enemy has retired along the whole of our front. Visited MONCHY. Enemy has left dynamite in dugouts and plenty of live bombs by attached to trip wires all over. No mans land and in MONCHY village. At 4.30 P.M. orders were received to withdraw whole company to billets at BAILEULMENT. RM Capt.	

WAR DIARY or INTELLIGENCE SUMMARY

Army Form C. 2118.

(Erase heading not required.)

Instructions regarding War Diaries and Intelligence Summaries are contained in F. S. Regs., Part II. and the Staff Manual respectively. Title Pages will be prepared in manuscript.

Place	Date 1917	Hour	Summary of Events and Information	Remarks and references to Appendices
BAILEULMENT	MAR. 19		All guns, tripods etc cleaned and thoroughly overhauled. Fighting limbers packed. Enemy still retiring on their HINDENBURG LINE. This Brigade is withdrawn to Divisional Reserve and remains as at present. H.Q. and M.G. Coy remain at BAILEULMENT. Fine during day — very heavy rain started about 5.P.M. RdM Capt.	
"	20		Limbers all packed ready to move. Company labour turned to POMMIER preparing stone. All guns tested and as many spare parts as possible completed. Fine — very strong W. wind. RdM Capt.	
"	21		Limbers marked and wheels greased. Marching Order inspection of whole company by O.C. at 5.P.M. Warning order received to be ready to move to POMMIER any time tomorrow.	

Army Form C. 2118.

WAR DIARY
INTELLIGENCE SUMMARY
(Erase heading not required.)

Instructions regarding War Diaries and Intelligence Summaries are contained in F. S. Regs., Part II. and the Staff Manual respectively. Title Pages will be prepared in manuscript.

Place	Date 1917	Hour	Summary of Events and Information	Remarks and references to Appendices
BAILEULMENT	MAR 22		Company marched off to POMMIER at 8.30 A.M. Billets occupied at POMMIER by 12 noon. Cold — wind N.W. RMCapt	
POMMIER	23		No 2 section marched to BOISLEUX au MONT — in reserve line. This section will proceed into the front line on 24-3-17 and will be in the left sector. Cold — wind mild — N.W. RMCapt	
	24		No III Section marched to HAMELINCOURT — in reserve line. No IV " " " — BOISLEUX au MONT — No II " " " BOIRY-BECQUERELLE — in front line. Transport is very difficult — to get up to the line owing to poor roads being in nearly all the roads. Pack mules can be taken up to the trenches. Water in left sector can be obtained from the River COJEUL which is pure. Water for right sector has to be taken there in water cart and by petrol tins. RMCapt	

WAR DIARY
—OR—
INTELLIGENCE SUMMARY

(Erase heading not required.)

Army Form C. 2118.

Instructions regarding War Diaries and Intelligence Summaries are contained in F. S. Regs., Part II. and the Staff Manual respectively. Title Pages will be prepared in manuscript.

Place	Date	Hour	Summary of Events and Information	Remarks and references to Appendices
POMMIER	MAR 25		Coy HQ. and No I section moved to HAMELINCOURT—arrived in front at 3.30 p.m. No III section moved to the front line in right section — all 4 guns along a railway embankment as emplacements had no dug-outs. Limbers can be taken right up to section H.Q. No I section carry dug-outs (German) in reserve line near Coy H.Q. Coy H.Q. is in 2 German dug-outs at S.E. end of HAMELINCOURT Village. Wind cold. R.M. Capt	
HAMELINCOURT	26		Orders received that 62 M.G. Coy and Reserve 199 M.G. Coy relieve dawn 27-3-17. 62 M.G. Coy arrived at Coy H.Q. at 6.30 p.m. on 26-3-17. No I section relieved and marched back to PUISIEUX POMMIER at 7.30 p.m. Section quiet. Rain. R.M. Capt	

WAR DIARY
INTELLIGENCE SUMMARY
(Erase heading not required.)

Army Form C. 2118.

Instructions regarding War Diaries and Intelligence Summaries are contained in F. S. Regs., Part II. and the Staff Manual respectively. Title Pages will be prepared in manuscript.

Place	Date 1917	Hour	Summary of Events and Information	Remarks and references to Appendices
HAMELIN-COURT	MAR 27		62 M.G. Coy relieved 198 M.G. Coy. Relief completed by 10 A.M. Coy marched back to POMMIER to each section dismounted. Occupied billets at POMMIER by 3.0 P.M. Fine day – mild N.W. wind. R.M.M. Capt.	
POMMIER	28		Remained at POMMIER. Cleaned up and fitted up men with boots, clothing etc as is possible. Returned Coy packed limbers. Fine weather. R.M.M. Capt.	
	29		Coy. marched with Batt. A. Bgw. by mined rd BOUT DES PRES and took over new gun positions at BOUT. DES. PRES. & and took over new gun positions in BOUT.DES.PRES. & and took over new gun positions. All ta. thro. All tactical schemes. Carried out 2 tactical schemes. Weather — wet and cold. R.M.M. Capt.	

WAR DIARY
or
INTELLIGENCE SUMMARY

(Erase heading not required.)

Army Form C. 2118.

Place	Date	Hour	Summary of Events and Information	Remarks and references to Appendices
BOUT-DES-PRES	MAR 30 1917	9.0	Company parade - clean fatigue dress.	
		9.30	Section parade - fitting clothing & boots.	
		12.30	Cleaning guns. All available officers met Capt. M.G.O. at HALLOY at 10 A.M. carried out practically the scheme thought out yesterday.	
			Weather - fine at intervals. Strong cold W. wind - South W.	R.O.M. Capt.
	31	8.0 to 12.30 p.m.	Sections paraded at 1 hour intervals and marched to baths at GROUCHES.	
		2.30	Sgt. majors parade - arms drill. Prepared to move to LIGNY tomorrow. Very wet day and cold N. wind.	R.O.M. Capt.

WAR DIARY Vol 5
198 Machine Gun Company.

VOLUME V

APRIL 1917

WAR DIARY / INTELLIGENCE SUMMARY

Army Form C. 2118.

Place	Date	Hour	Summary of Events and Information	Remarks and references to Appendices
BOUT DES PRES	1917 APR 1	8 Am	Company marched with Transport to LIGNY-sur-CANCHE. Column consisted of R.E.s, M.G.C. and F.Amb. Arrived LIGNY about 2 P.M. Billets occupied by 2.30 P.M. Mules tied to Lines here in the Road. Billets very good for officers and men. Fine Day.	RM Capt
LIGNY	2	8.15	Company paraded and marched to join Column at G.H.Q. marched with B.H.Q. to FONTAINE L'ETALON. Just followed direct from BOUT DES-PRES to FONTAINE on April 1st and arranged billets. Owing to being the first billeting party very attractive excellent billets. All mules and horses in stables in covered standings. Company occupied billets at 2.30 P.M. Fine Day — rather cold.	RM Capt

Army Form C. 2118.

WAR DIARY
or
INTELLIGENCE SUMMARY

(Erase heading not required.)

Instructions regarding War Diaries and Intelligence Summaries are contained in F. S. Regs., Part II. and the Staff Manual respectively. Title Pages will be prepared in manuscript.

Place	Date	Hour	Summary of Events and Information	Remarks and references to Appendices
FONTAINE L'ETALON	APR 3	10 AM	Company Inspection - Clean fatigue dress. Reports in respect of limbers and been given etc. It was arranged that company moves out to Ya BEAUMILLE. Snow and rain - rather cold. Pte Bourke (No 2 Section) died last night in his billet of it. He was buried in churchyard of village. Church RM dept	
	4	9:30 AM	Transport left with 14th Bde. Transport for AMPLIS under Lieut Potter.	
		9:30	Company paraded full marching order with 2 blankets to two AL buses. Buses and lorries arrived at 11:0 AM. Company packed into 6 buses + very lit & lorries. Lorries departed at 1:0 PM & proceeded via DOULLENS to MAILLY-MAILLET. Arrived at 5:45 PM. In billets arranged. Company was eventually accommodated in Huts in No 2 Camp. Returned cold day. RM dept	

WAR DIARY
INTELLIGENCE SUMMARY
(Erase heading not required.)

Army Form C. 2118.

Place	Date	Hour	Summary of Events and Information	Remarks and references to Appendices
MAILLY- MAILLET.	1917 APR. 5	10 AM	Company Inspection - clean fatigue dress. Re-clothing of huts - and stores. Fixing up stables for horses and mules. Sections unpacking limbers. RDM Capt Showery Day.	
	6		Sections paraded for gun drill and I.A. Sgt. Magnus paraded. 198 in & coy detailed to proceed to ACHIET-LE-GRAND to erect huts and act as advance party to the Bele Tomorrow. 	
		2 PM 10.30 PM	Sent for by Bele Major R.O.C. Thornton races etc. next week M G Coy to go up with the Bele to make roads in Railways. Brigade moves to ACHIET-LE-GRAND to make roads. 2/t in Bn and 19 P M G Coy remain at MAILLET. The Bn finds working parties here and meantime training. Very cold wind.	RDM Capt RDM Capt

WAR DIARY
INTELLIGENCE SUMMARY

Army Form C. 2118.

Place	Date	Hour	Summary of Events and Information	Remarks and references to Appendices
MAILLY	APR 8 1917	AM 10.30	Parade for service in Y.M.C.A. Hut at 11.0 A.M. All blankets hung on trees and aired. All men ordered to wash their change of clothing. RQM Capt Fine warm day	
	9	7.0 9.0 2.0	Running & PT Section parades for inspection, practice & gun drills. 2 lecturing marched to SERRE to have explained to them system of German trenches and wire/trails. Hacking Water. Cookery and tool armt. RQM Capt	
	10	7.0 9.0	Running & PT Parades and huts owing to snow + rain Weather Alternate snow and sunshine. RQM Capt	

WAR DIARY
INTELLIGENCE SUMMARY
(Erase heading not required.)

Army Form C. 2118.

Instructions regarding War Diaries and Intelligence Summaries are contained in F. S. Regs., Part II. and the Staff Manual respectively. Title Pages will be prepared in manuscript.

Place	Date 1917	Hour	Summary of Events and Information	Remarks and references to Appendices
MAILLY M	Apr 11	7.0 9.0 2.0P	Running & P.T. Section parades for Prodder practice and M.G. Work. Sgt Majors Parade — saluting etc RDM Capt Weather. Cold — showery	
—	12	A.m 9.0	Company Paraded — full marching order. Marched to ACHIET-LE-GRAND via MIRAUMENT. On arrival pitched tents (12) and shelters (60) in a field. Continued to rain hard on our arrival (about 3 PM) and continued all night. RDM Capt	
BIHUCOURT	13		Spent morning collecting wood from village of BIHUCOURT to provide floorboards and improve shelters. Built a Mens Hut and commenced a harness room. Weather — fine and sunny. RDM Capt	
—	14	7.6 AM 9.0 AM 2.0 PM	Sgt Majors Parade Section Parades — cleaning up and M.G. Work Weather still fine — ground drying up. RDM Capt	

Army Form C. 2118.

WAR DIARY
or
INTELLIGENCE SUMMARY
(Erase heading not required.)

Instructions regarding War Diaries and Intelligence Summaries are contained in F. S. Regs., Part II. and the Staff Manual respectively. Title Pages will be prepared in manuscript.

Place	Date 1917	Hour	Summary of Events and Information	Remarks and references to Appendices
BIHUCOURT	15		About 7.30 A.M. a large shell burst 400 yds from camp. Until 8.15 A.M. 12cm large shells arrived — they traversed across valley. Nearest camp is 6 cm. les from line. They must have large calibre. No damage was done. The company had to assist filling in the shell holes to prevent them being photographed from the air. Pieces of one shell we found, they were 28 cm. shells. The base of one shell was found. Very fine and sunny weather.	R.O.M Capt.
	16		Company found working party of 90 men last night and supplied same for next two nights. Paraded 6.30 P.M. and marched to VAULX-VRAUCOURT — arrived back in camp about 3.0 A.M. Weather — wet and windy.	R.O.M Capt.

WAR DIARY
or
INTELLIGENCE SUMMARY

Army Form C. 2118.

(Erase heading not required.)

Instructions regarding War Diaries and Intelligence Summaries are contained in F. S. Regs., Part II. and the Staff Manual respectively. Title Pages will be prepared in manuscript.

Place	Date	Hour	Summary of Events and Information	Remarks and references to Appendices
BIHUCOURT	Apr. 17 1917		Scheme arranged for Nos I. II. IV Sections to take up positions in 3rd line of defence – Coys M.G.O. was coming round to inspect. Two met for this scheme.	
		2.30 PM	Coys M.G.O. inspected Sections on parade. No I Section – pack saddlery. No IV – small tactical scheme. He sent a report in the company. Training being carried out on sound lines – officers knew their work – men have good knowledge but require more practice.	
	18		Nos I II & IV Sections manned 3rd line of defence in position by 12 noon – positions inspected and necessary alterations made. Arrived back in Camp 2.30 P.M Weather – cloudy – not raining.	

RM Capt.

Army Form C. 2118.

WAR DIARY
or
INTELLIGENCE SUMMARY

(Erase heading not required.)

Instructions regarding War Diaries and Intelligence Summaries are contained in F. S. Regs., Part II. and the Staff Manual respectively. Title Pages will be prepared in manuscript.

Place	Date	Hour	Summary of Events and Information	Remarks and references to Appendices
BIAUCOURT	1917 April 19	7.0	Sgt Majors Parade	
		9.0	Section Parades — Machine gun practice. Advancing in open country.	
		2.0 PM	—	
			Weather — warmer — cloudy. RM Capt.	
	20		1 Section detailed to supply 4 guns for anti-aircraft duty. 2 mounted in trench near camp — 2 mounted at far end of Puzzle Camp. Sentry on duty for each pair of guns during hours of daylight. Sections carried out training in Pack Battery — advancing in open country etc. Weather — dull — colder. RM Capt.	
	21	7.0	Sgt Major Parade	
		9.0	Company Inspection — fighting order	
		2 PM	Section Parades.	
			Weather — sunny — cool wind. RM Capt.	

Army Form C. 2118.

WAR DIARY
or
INTELLIGENCE SUMMARY
(Erase heading not required.)

Instructions regarding War Diaries and Intelligence Summaries are contained in F. S. Regs., Part II. and the Staff Manual respectively. Title Pages will be prepared in manuscript.

Place	Date 1917	Hour	Summary of Events and Information	Remarks and references to Appendices
BIHUCOURT	April 22	7.0. 11.0 AM	Sgt Majors Parade. Company Parade in Church Parade in Brigade Headquarters. The following officers of this company received promotion to Temp. Lieutenant (dated Jan. 1st 1917) 2nd Lt E.G. Fricker (East Sur. Regt) T/2nd Lt H. Dutton. T/2nd Lt E.V. Laurie. RSM Capt.	
"	23	7.0 9.0	Sgt Majors Parade. Section Parades - open fighting. Weather - dull and cold. RSM Capt.	
"	24	7.0 9.0	Sgt Majors Parade. Company Paraded with limbers fighting order. Marched off towards 90MIE COURT. Scheme in which company carried out in front of 90MIE COURT. Returned to Camp at 2.0 PM. Weather fine. RSM Capt.	

Army Form C. 2118.

WAR DIARY
or
INTELLIGENCE SUMMARY
(Erase heading not required.)

Instructions regarding War Diaries and Intelligence Summaries are contained in F. S. Regs., Part II. and the Staff Manual respectively. Title Pages will be prepared in manuscript.

Place	Date 1917	Hour	Summary of Events and Information	Remarks and references to Appendices
BIHUCOURT	APR 25	7.0	Sgt Majors Parade. Sections paraded for Baths at 1 hour intervals.	
		9.10. 12 noon	Section Parades. Weather fine & sunny - wind fresh N.E. RMCapt	
		2.0		
	26	7.0	Sgt Majors Parade.	
		9.0	Company paraded for inspection - fighting order.	
		9.30	Section parades - Parkesolling etc.	
		2.0	Section Parades. Weather fine & sunny. Wind slight. N. RMCapt.	
	27	7.0AM	Sgt Majors Parade.	
		9.0	Company Parade - fighting order with Transport. Marched to square G.12.d. Took up positions in co-operation with imaginary infantry. Weather fine & wind from N. RMCapt.	

Army Form C. 2118.

WAR DIARY
or
INTELLIGENCE SUMMARY
(Erase heading not required.)

Instructions regarding War Diaries and Intelligence Summaries are contained in F. S. Regs., Part II, and the Staff Manual respectively. Title Pages will be prepared in manuscript.

Place	Date	Hour	Summary of Events and Information	Remarks and references to Appendices
BIHUCOURT	1917 APR. 28	7.0	Sgt majors parade. Communication drill to form N.C.O.s.	
		9.0	Section parades — taking up positions — practice firing Z.	
		2.0	—	
			Weather fine. Wind N.W. R.M.Capt	
	29.	7.0	Company parade — clean fatigue dress — cleaning camp	
		11.10	Church Parade — for service in Brigade Headquarters	
			Weather fine. Wind light N.E. R.M.Capt	
	30.	7.0	Sgt majors Parade	
		9.0	Company inspection — fighting order. Then section Parades.	
		2.0	Sect on parade	
			Weather fine. Wind fresh N.E. R.M.Capt	

SECRET.   Volume VI

WAR DAIRY.
198th Machine Gun Company
for the Month of May 1917.

Army Form C. 2118.

WAR DIARY
or
INTELLIGENCE SUMMARY
(Erase heading not required.)

Instructions regarding War Diaries and Intelligence Summaries are contained in F. S. Regs., Part II. and the Staff Manual respectively. Title Pages will be prepared in manuscript.

Place	Date	Hour	Summary of Events and Information	Remarks and references to Appendices
BIHUCOURT	MAR 1	7:0 9:0	Sgt Majors Parade. Inspection of kits and shelters — Afterwards Section parades — stoppages — I.A. pack paddings etc. EDM Capt.	
	2	10am 9:0	Sgt Majors Parade. Section paraded under S.Os — small tactical schemes in preparation to joining with Bn H in schemes. EDM Capt.	
	3	10am 9:0	Sgt Majors Parade. Full marching order inspection. Tactical scheme for section in contact with transport and park guides. Also the sun — hot. EDM Capt.	
	4	10am 9:0 9:0	Sgt Majors parade. Whole Company paraded for everything worth reporting ult afternoon — Pit sh. made up. Sect In cmder EDM Capt	

2449 Wt. W14957/M90 750,000 1/16 J.B.C. & A. Forms/C.2118/12.

WAR DIARY or INTELLIGENCE SUMMARY

Army Form C. 2118.

Place	Date	Hour	Summary of Events and Information	Remarks and references to Appendices
BIHUCOURT	May 5		All Bn. holding Bivouac offensive fatigue parties for Engineers intensive training. M.G. sections preparing small tactical schemes for cooperation with Bren in field work. H.M. Coy.	
	6		Refer to List. Letters to accompany in training. All four sections headquarters and transport to field exhibition for 2 hours. Officers and NCOs of platoon carried on section training as the list. H.M. Coy.	
	7		Day & Night parades return parades. At 6.30 pm orders were received that B Coy Bn. was ordered to proceed via Bn. HQ position at BAPAUME – BIHUCOURT Rd at dawn and join the OP patrol of 17 Bn. to hold present line. Companies moved with 2/5... 2/6... to take position a head 2/R. in Reserve. Operations of patrol commenced 4.30 at 1.30 AM orders to fall in another position. H.M. Coy.	

WAR DIARY or INTELLIGENCE SUMMARY

Army Form C. 2118.

Place	Date	Hour	Summary of Events and Information	Remarks and references to Appendices
In the Field	8/5/17	7AM	Company & Coy. Paraded for Running and P.T.	
		9AM	Section Parades - Throwing German Grenades, Gun drill & Stokes artillery.	
		2PM	ditto — Overhauling Guns and spare parts	
		3.30PM	all Limbers washed and cleaned. Captains Messing Commanding the Company paraded the Company	
	9/5/17	7AM	Company in Camp. Paraded for Run and P.T.	
		7AM	Company parade. Practice - flight order of a Brigade Tactical Scheme	
		2PM	Sections paraded and practiced Gun drill and T.A. 2nd Lieut	
			weather remaining warm and fine.	
	10/5/17	7AM	Company & Coy. Paraded for running and P.T.	
		9AM	Sections prepare Limbers for Bde Tactical Scheme tomorrow	
		4PM	Practice of Bde Tactical Scheme. Brigade attack on Lowpart Wood. 57CMA 6349 35. 2nd Lieut.	

WAR DIARY
or
INTELLIGENCE SUMMARY

Army Form C. 2118.

Place	Date	Hour	Summary of Events and Information	Remarks and references to Appendices
Little Guiluff	13/2/17	11.9 AM	Brigade Tactical Scheme. Guns practical push forward to fire consolidation. Ammunition supply etc. A very instructive exercise. Return to Camp at 4.30 PM. Day warm + fine.	
	14/2/17	7 AM	Company in Camp. Parade for Running and P.T.	
		9 AM	Section Parade. Gun drill - Gas outrages - aiming at Bretelu in throwing grenades.	
		2 PM	Sections Parade. Gun drill & musketry.	
	15/2/17	9 AM	Inspection by V Corps M.G.O. Equipment and Transport up to date and complete. Cyclo M.G. & 9 musketleb sections at work. Result - very favourable impression.	
		2 PM	Sections overhaul guns etc. Warm order received for 7th Division to proceed to BULLECOURT and relieve a Bde of the 7th Division 14/15/7th. Probable time midnight	

WAR DIARY
or
INTELLIGENCE SUMMARY

(Erase heading not required.)

Army Form C. 2118.

Place	Date 1917	Hour	Summary of Events and Information	Remarks and references to Appendices
In the field	May 9th	7am.	Sgt Majors Parade in Camp.	
		9am.	Sections paraded at 9 AM. After inspection sections carried out small tactical schemes, viz MacRimmons in open fighting etc.	
		2.30 to 4 pm	Squad drill under NCOs and inspections.	

[signature] Lieut.

WAR DIARY
or
INTELLIGENCE SUMMARY

(Erase heading not required.)

Army Form C. 2118.

Instructions regarding War Diaries and Intelligence Summaries are contained in F. S. Regs., Part II. and the Staff Manual respectively. Title Pages will be prepared in manuscript.

Place	Date 1917	Hour	Summary of Events and Information	Remarks and references to Appendices
BULLECOURT	MAY 15	9 AM	Packing gun equipment in limbers preparing for move.	
		2 PM	Moved to camp at SAPIGNIES. R.M. Capt	
SAPIGNIES	16	5 PM	Company moved to MORY MORMAL to take over new line at 5 P.M.	
			2 Sect. took over active line from 22 M.G. Coy.	
		8.30 PM	2 — moved up to BULLECOURT with all material except gun no. mounts & infantry were paraded. From ECOUST to BULLECOURT gun no. mounts & ammunition were paraded. From ECOUST to BULLECOURT guns were exhausted on arrival at BULLECOURT. Lieut Smith (19 M.G. Coy) who had gone on in advance met the officer & informed them that an attack was taking place at 2 A.M. 17-5-17. Relief had to be postponed.	
MORT HOMME	17	5 AM	The attack being successful the relief was carried out. In consequence of the leaving of village dispositions of guns had to be altered. A gun was mounted for cover to protect SOUTH and WEST sides of village. All guns now in their new positions. Enemy snipers & trench otherwise quiet. Small parties of Germans seen in O21.c.8.0 R.M. Capt	

WAR DIARY or INTELLIGENCE SUMMARY

Army Form C. 2118.

Place	Date	Hour	Summary of Events and Information	Remarks and references to Appendices
MORT HOMME	1917 May 18		Enemy continued to shell HINDENBURG LINE & village mostly with 5.9". Infantry constructed a strong point at CRUCIFIX and new covered E.M.G. was placed in this position. 2Lt M Capt'd	
			BULLE COURT was shelled intermittently throughout day	
	19	2 PM	Sections were relieved by 2 secs of same company. Immediately after relief a bombardment took place. J'T LING dugout was hit — Wooden village was hit in the back by a piece of shell — though not badly. 2 LT FRICKEE took command of the whole BULLE COURT sector. During the night the gun at CRUCIFIX was put out of action and withdrawn. 2Lt M Capt'd	
	20		2/Lt LESSER relieved Lt FRICKER. Digging day. Village was very heavily shelled. Enemy placed a own Barrage in evening. The gun team in U.21 B.1 suffered heavy casualties by German shell bursting a gas cylinder. 3 men died of gas poisoning and 2 others bad to hospital in a serious condition. Cpl Goode, although suffering badly would not leave his gun till relieved by the Brigade forwarded this. 2Lt M Capt'd	
			NEW name for D.C.M. ERITH in a target gun in U.21 A.2.7 was killed — 4 men wounded. The gun was knocked off its mounting. 2Lt M Capt'd	

WAR DIARY or INTELLIGENCE SUMMARY

Army Form C. 2118.

Place	Date	Hour	Summary of Events and Information	Remarks and references to Appendices
MORT HOMME	20/21		During night another m[achine] Bors TRENCH together with crews 2/Lt Bry, L/Cpl AMY, Cpts 24 LESSER was despatched by Lieufenant? and an infantry party point before the gun could reach the strongpoint a barrage was put down & gun could not get forward. 24 LESSER took up position in shell hole and worked gun. The team was supposed to be very heavy fire handled both by German big [?] shells + immediate from handmghts - by Lft Lft ... 24 LESSER made a reconnaissance and attacked attention of garrison of a strongpoint. The whole team gradually received strong fire with the gun + eventually it [?] infantry chaps refused. Hit. Meso gun + Rifling Sgt Twoley + Pte Statler Pte Belts to was wounded. R/M Cpt Reinforcements arrived with a new gun and position was again held Laving night Butte court was heavily bombarded and [?] barrel 82 men were wounded R/M Cpt	

WAR DIARY or INTELLIGENCE SUMMARY

Army Form C. 2118.

Place	Date 1917	Hour	Summary of Events and Information	Remarks and references to Appendices
MORT HOMME	MAR 22		Lt REID and 2/Lt LESSER were relieved and some of the men by some men of the company. Situation fairly quiet. Day was fairly quiet.	POM apt
	23		Company in the line was relieved by 214 M.G. Company. 2 Lieutenants went out to camp at Transport Lines MORT and 2 sections remained in YELLOW LINE at MORT HOMME.	POM apt
	24		Whole day spent in reorganising sections and fitting out deficiencies. All deficiencies were immediately indented for — these amounted mostly of spare parts, belt boxes & 2 guns incomplete.	POM apt
	25		Whole company was put on a working party at YRANCOURT — relieving 67 and M.G. Corps Reconnte. S'LEGER (YELLOW) Line.	POM apt
	26		7 guns were armed as a draft. The working party for this company cancelled to allow company to fit out new equipment etc. 2 guns put on YELLOW LINE 2 g' natural dismounted for A.A. work	POM apt

WAR DIARY or INTELLIGENCE SUMMARY

Army Form C. 2118.

Place	Date 1917	Hour	Summary of Events and Information	Remarks and references to Appendices
MORT HOMME	MAR 27		2 Bns of the Brigade placed into the line in right and centre in the ny't of BULLECOURT. 7 gun teams (N°I Sect'n - 3 teams from N°II Sect) prepared to go into this sect early next morning.	
	28		7 gun teams went into the line in right and centre in front line – 4 in support line & 2 in reserve. In almost embankment sector. In this sector we held 4 MEEMSTer 9 emplacements but Temporarily mounted Punchel plant in parts of the line. Good dug outs. N° MG compliments at all Stations save 1 in open night position em bankment.	
	29		Handed over the positions in YELLOW wing to 208 M.G. Company and the section went into Camp at Transport lines MORY. Remaining 3 crew of N°IV Section & N°II Sect prepared to go into the line at BULLECOURT.	
	30		Took over 5 gun positions in BULLECOURT from 2/4 M.G. Coy. Transferred on village, all gt'ly improved by this Coy – nearly all gun positions have been spotted and one rd. by enemy. Og of comp'd on reconoft'ly. The thing made up.	

R.J.M.Ropert

Place	Date	Hour	Summary of Events and Information	Remarks and references to Appendices
MORT HOMME	1917 MAR 31		Reinforcements 1 officer and 10 men arrived from base. Wilhelm line (empty) in flight out of artl'y. arrived at my arty gun position – 2 guns in action for rest. Nearly all work has to be done at night. Situation quiet during day – moderate shelling at night chiefly in BULLECOURT. MMCapt	

1917

SECRET.

198th Machine Gun Company.

WAR DIARY. VOLUME VII.

JUNE. 1917.

WAR DIARY
INTELLIGENCE SUMMARY
(Erase heading not required.)

Army Form C. 2118.

Place	Date	Hour	Summary of Events and Information	Remarks and references to Appendices
MONT HOMME	1917 June 1		Lt LING & 3 gun teams of N° 3 Sect relieved 2 M.G. teams of N°1 Sect in right sub-sector — one gun in front line and 2 in support line. Our own artillery opened flight trench bombardment at 10.30 pm in preparation for a slight bombing raid. The enemy replied about 10.50 pm with a fairly heavy barrage along support line and at BULLECOURT. Nevertheless the relief was carried out successfully with no casualties. N°1 Sect had one casualty in early morning. Lee Cpl WOOD was cleaning gun in trench just after dismounting gun when he was hit in arm, leg, and side. This appeared to be not dangerous. Weather — fine and hot. R.M. Capt.	

WAR DIARY
or
INTELLIGENCE SUMMARY

(Erase heading not required.)

Army Form C. 2118.

Instructions regarding War Diaries and Intelligence Summaries are contained in F. S. Regs., Part II. and the Staff Manual respectively. Title Pages will be prepared in manuscript.

Place	Date	Hour	Summary of Events and Information	Remarks and references to Appendices
MORT HOMME	June 2		16 Tudgin teams made up from M.G. coy in reserve went to BULLECOURT to relieve 2 teams of No II section. Everything very quiet indeed during relief – a full moon made almost daylight must say. The right hand gun in BULLECOURT was much from position in sunken [lane?] had very little field of fire in [several?] [directions?] but was replaced by 9 June to put [line?] in [...] [...]. [...] to [...] BULLECOURT was [...] by [...] [...] [...] of 2 [...] [...] [...] [...] [...] sharp [storm?] about 7pm. 1st & 2nd Relief sections [arriving?] to sections 20 at BULLECOURT to get Tower and idea of the [ground] [...] to [...] [...] on their way up from [...] to [...] 2 sections from 215 MG Coy [...] [...] [...] [...] [...] No 356th (Goods) C.E. 188 M.G. Company awarded the Military Medal for bringing up two carts of ammunition & his gun crew & all the team had become [...] at BULLECOURT. This is the first award one of this company [...] had [...]. [R.M. Capt.]	

Army Form C. 2118.

WAR DIARY
or
INTELLIGENCE SUMMARY
(Erase heading not required.)

Instructions regarding War Diaries and Intelligence Summaries are contained in F. S. Regs., Part II. and the Staff Manual respectively. Title Pages will be prepared in manuscript.

Place	Date 1917	Hour	Summary of Events and Information	Remarks and references to Appendices
MONT HOMME	May 4	2.15	12 teams of 2.15 M.T. Coy relieved the 12 teams of 143 M.T. Coy which were in the line. Relief completed at 1.39 A.M. 5-5-17. Company was in camp at MORT with the transport. Coy H.Q. left MONT HOMME for MORT at 8.P.M. Weather fine and hot.	fkm/Capt
MORT	5		Morning spent in checking equipment of guns and men also cleaning up. All deficiencies indented for at once. A few shells were fired at the camp during the day and evening. Only 2 were in the camp. No damage was done. About 10.30 P.M. an aeroplane flew over the camp and dropped about 6 bombs all of which exploded near the camp. No damage was done. Weather - fine and very hot.	

Army Form C. 2118.

WAR DIARY
INTELLIGENCE SUMMARY.
(Erase heading not required.)

Instructions regarding War Diaries and Intelligence Summaries are contained in F.S. Regs., Part II. and the Staff Manual respectively. Title pages will be prepared in manuscript.

Place	Date 1917	Hour	Summary of Events and Information	Remarks and references to Appendices
MORT	June 6.	7. 9.0	Sgt Majors Parade in Camp Lecture Parade. IA Made myself limited my Batt - Coffee at MORT. RQM Capt.	
	7	7 9.0 12.30	Made myself fit and very hot Sgt Major's Parade in Camp Bath Parades. Special attention being paid to impecunious IA and I.k is the other if many men here been very fit RQM Capt.	
	8	7.0 9.0	Sgt Majors Parade Section Parades. 2 N.C. O's attend Divisional Gas Course for 3 Days. (a) 10.30 P.M. 5 of 7th aeroplanes different officer every day in neighbourhood of camp dropped a few bombs No damage done. RQM Capt.	

WAR DIARY
INTELLIGENCE SUMMARY

Army Form C. 2118.

Place	Date	Hour	Summary of Events and Information	Remarks and references to Appendices
Moar	June 9 1917	6.	Sgt Majors Parade. Usual Parades. Sent Sgt M.T. S.M. + 2 other ranks preceded on leave to U.K. Doctor not fine.	
"	10	11:-	Company Paraded for Church Parade. Went to together with 2 guns of N.Z. Sect proceeded to embankment behind Battle Court, under command of Lieut Tricker. 4 guns of No IV Sect with 2 guns of No III Sect opposed to against No III Sect with 2 guns of No III Sect & No IV Sect proceeded to embankment in V.2.5. d model Lieut Smith. Flex guns on hostile barrage in enemy front line 150 of Zoo dugh & that of L.V. 17.3. BE an enemy of 12 Bn — camp got terribly flooded. Terrific thunderstorm — camp got terribly flooded. R M Paget	

WAR DIARY
or
INTELLIGENCE SUMMARY.

Army Form C. 2118.

Place	Date	Hour	Summary of Events and Information	Remarks and references to Appendices
MERT	June 1917 11.		O.Ha. R.ly. 173 Bde postponed for at least 3 days. Head of gun train on Lumberment Tunnel to arrive by daylight. 3 lines of twenty a pieces and collected at knight. RDM Capt	
"	12.		Bde held in readiness to relieve 173 Bde in left sector. Section function. Relief starting half yearly. Water pure. RDM Capt	
"	13.		Advanced left sector report ore 20.6 M.G. by to become augmented with gun positions. Covers a ration embankment and 2 forward. YM Capt	

Place	Date	Hour	Summary of Events and Information	Remarks and references to Appendices
MORT	July June 14		Same guns & were detailed on 11-6-17 prepared to go into emplacement again for barrage on morning of 15th. Permission of gun not 2 limited to proceed by daylight to ECOUST carrying guns and tripods. All 3 gun teams OR reached their positions safely. Weather fine.	
	15		The 12 guns on embankment put up heavy barrage from 2.50 A.M to 3.5 A.M. The attack then took place by 173 - 1 Bde. Objectives gained. 1 Casualty to teams of barrage guns — man hit by piece of shell — evacuated. Very quiet during rest of the day. 9.30 P.M. our S.O.S. was sent up — Probably wind up only. M.G.s fired for 10 minutes on their old targets. Same again at 11 P.M.	

P.M. Oot.

WAR DIARY
or
INTELLIGENCE SUMMARY.
(Erase heading not required.)

Army Form C. 2118.

Place	Date	Hour	Summary of Events and Information	Remarks and references to Appendices
MORP	16	-	Enemy put fairly heavy barrage of 5.9" on embankment most of night - very heavy between 12mn & 1 A.M. Also strong at 2.45 A.M. 3.10 A.M. M.G. Barrage opened on old targets for 15 minutes. Each gun fired 8 boxes except 1 which had separated case which could not be extracted from breech. Our S.O.S. again put up at 4.0 A.M. Enemy shelling ceased about ZERO (3.10 A.M.) and at 4.30 A.M. conditions were normal.	
MORP	17	-	Total guns left section from 206 M.G. Coy. 6 guns in first line - 6 guns on Embankment. Of first line 6 consists of old Hindenburg front line except in extreme left it is Nieuwied and in many cases it is flat. Contains very strong concrete emplacements & dug-outs (MEBUS) none of which have been cracked up.	

WAR DIARY
or
INTELLIGENCE SUMMARY.
(Erase heading not required.)

Army Form C. 2118.

Place	Date	Hour	Summary of Events and Information	Remarks and references to Appendices
MORY	June 1917 17(cont)		3 guns are in left of post line where trench is good. The trench line in trench itself 2 guns in MEBUS where trench is bad. 1 gun in MEBUS where — is very bad. The only way to visit the right 3 guns is by short and sharp rushes along what once was trench. During relief Sgt Wilcox was wounded while on his way to right B gun. Relief completed successfully. R.M Capt.	
to VRAUCOURT ST LEGER (end B.Ad)	18	7	The MEBUS in which H.L. ESSER lies with 2 gun teams contains 9 wounded who have been there 4 days. Bde arranged for Lyn. Watering party to take these away during night. Unable to get Sgt Wilcox down last night. H LESSER made several attempts to evacuate 2 infantry stretcher bearers were wounded. Infantry party sent. R.M Capt.	

WAR DIARY
or
INTELLIGENCE SUMMARY.
(Erase heading not required.)

Army Form C. 2118.

Place	Date	Hour	Summary of Events and Information	Remarks and references to Appendices
B.11.d.1.9.	27 June 19		During last night dgt Mcleod was brought down to RAP and thence evacuated to CCS. He was hit by shrapnel in both legs. Everything fairly quiet. In the evening 2/Lt Dutton & Lt Bartley with 6 teams relieved Lt Reid & 2/Lt Lower and their teams who marched off. 2/Lt B Transport Lines at MORT. RDM Capt	
— " —	20		Went H/ Lt Pollings to sunken road at top of PELICAN AVENUE to reconnoitre a position for a gun. The ground from there looks all down valley German lines are considerable distant observation. not less than 600 away. Hostile gun in till — firing RDM Capt and placed at top of PELICAN AVENUE Digg out + emplacement have to be made by team. Station very quiet. RDM Capt	

WAR DIARY
or
INTELLIGENCE SUMMARY.

(Erase heading not required.)

Army Form C. 2118.

Place	Date	Hour	Summary of Events and Information	Remarks and references to Appendices
B.4.d	June 21		91st L.Bde to relieve 174 L.Bde m.zng.Lt 23/24 —	
			91 M.G.Coy " " 24/25 —	
			Major Gatchey O.C 91 M.G.Coy came round line with one to see positions.	
			Situation very quiet.	
			R.M. Capt	
"	22		Reconnoitred a position along support line for a gun. Support line covers merely of a line of infantry posts sometimes with a Lewis Gun. The only one suitable for a M.G. was L.8. From this post direct hits can be obtained on valley to N of BULLECOURT. An enemy mobile gun of 3 left guns of first line was in the area and placed in this post.	
			Situation normal.	
			R.M. Capt	

WAR DIARY
or
INTELLIGENCE SUMMARY.
(Erase heading not required.)

Army Form C. 2118.

Place	Date 1917	Hour	Summary of Events and Information	Remarks and references to Appendices
B.4.d.	June 23		Visited gun position in L8 post and laid the guns by aiming level on Hindenburg support line. Arranged about relief tomorrow. About 6. P.M enemy put some 4.2' and few 5.9' on fields in front of By H.Q. This continued at irregular intervals until about 7.30 P.M. Situation normal. RM Capt.	
B.4.d.	24	8.0am	3 gun teams 91 M.G. Coy proceeded to relieve 3 teams of 257 ESSER	
		1.PM	3 more teams 91 M.G Coy proceeded to relieve remainder of 198 M.G Coy. Relief completed by 2. AM 25/6/17. Teams so relieved marched to renew rest lines at MORY.	JM Capt

Army Form C. 2118.

WAR DIARY
— or —
INTELLIGENCE SUMMARY.
(Erase heading not required.)

Instructions regarding War Diaries and Intelligence Summaries are contained in F. S. Regs., Part II. and the Staff Manual respectively. Title pages will be prepared in manuscript.

Place	Date	Hour	Summary of Events and Information	Remarks and references to Appendices
MLt	June 25 1916		Whole company spent day cleaning up and resting and packing stores ready to move tomorrow. R.M.Capt	
	26	10.0 AM	Company paraded ready to move to COURCELLES. Marched off 10.10. Arrived COURCELLES at 12 noon. Very good camp in field - officers tents in an orchard. R.M.Capt.	
COURCELLES	27	7.0 AM 9.0 AM	Sgt-Maj's Parade. Redistribution of equipment guns, belt boxes etc. to all sections - cleaning stores - fuse. Gun drill and 2 hour minstrels. Enemy shelled COURCELLES station in morning slightly. R.M.Capt.	
	28		Examined every man of Io. II sections in stoppages on range. Weather fine and very hot. R.M.Capt.	

Army Form C. 2118.

WAR DIARY
or
INTELLIGENCE SUMMARY.
(Erase heading not required.)

Instructions regarding War Diaries and Intelligence Summaries are contained in F. S. Regs., Part II. and the Staff Manual respectively. Title pages will be prepared in manuscript.

Place	Date 1917	Hour	Summary of Events and Information	Remarks and references to Appendices
COURCELLES	June 29	6.30AM	Sgt. Majors Parade	
		9.0	Examined every man of 3rd Section in stoppages. Formed class for extra instruction at 6 P.M. daily for such men as did not pass examination. Trod-miles & dinners for riding & driving competitions. RMCapt.	
	30	6.30AM	Sgt. Majors Parade — drill and P.T.	
		9.0	Section Parades — sword drill, gun drill etc. RMCapt. Weather — dull and rainy	

WAR DIARY
of
198 M.G. Coy.
1/7/17 to 31/7/17

WAR DIARY
INTELLIGENCE SUMMARY.
(Erase heading not required.)

Army Form C. 2118.

Place	Date	Hour	Summary of Events and Information	Remarks and references to Appendices
COURCELLES	1 Feb 1917	8.30am	Company paraded for Church Service in COURCELLES Theatre. Weather fine. RMCapt	
	2	2.30pm	Company paraded for route march - Transport taken. Marching Order. Route COURCELLES - MAGENVILLE - AYETTE - ABLAINZEVILLE - COURCELLES. Men conducted well - no straggllers. Weather fine. RMCapt	
	3	6.3a	Sgt Major's Parade	
		9.0	Section Parades. Stoppages - firing - gun drill	
		2.0	Bde Transport Sports. 198 M.G. Coy. won 1st Prize for limber driving (2 limbers) - L/Cpl Tolley - Dr Bainton. Team entered for M.T. Race - H. Pallier won 2nd prize in Bending Race. Weather fine. RMCapt	

WAR DIARY
INTELLIGENCE SUMMARY.
(Erase heading not required.)

Army Form C. 2118.

Place	Date	Hour	Summary of Events and Information	Remarks and references to Appendices
COURCELLES	July 1917 4	6.30	Running & P.T. from N.C.O's class	
		9.0?	Section parades under section officers	
		1.0 PM	Limbers harness cleaned in readiness for G.O.C. inspection. Weather fine.	A/M Capt
			Lt Buick & myself went to Ellis by motor bus to look for a line in which we shall take over in Sieges future. Everything seemed very quiet.	
	5	9.0 AM	Section Officers parades for sections.	
		10.0		
		11.15	Company parade full M.O. Appears for inspection	
		5.15 PM	Company inspected on parade by G.O.C. 58 Division Inspection satisfactory	

R.M Capt

WAR DIARY
INTELLIGENCE SUMMARY.
(Erase heading not required.)

Army Form C. 2118.

Place	Date 1917	Hour	Summary of Events and Information	Remarks and references to Appendices
COURCELLES	July 6		Morning spent in cleaning & packing limbers, drawing tents & shelters to dump.	
			Company packed at 5.4 5 PM to move there - marching order.	
			Marched via SAPIGNIES - BAPAUME - to BANCOURT.	
			1 man fell out but managed to finish.	
			Company accommodated in tents & shelters for night. R.M. Capt	
BANCOURT	7		Reconnoitred new line with Brigadier General.	
			Most M.G. positions seem useless - no field of fire at all.	
			All in support line actual front lines in the of resistance.	
			Company marched camp at FINS (V.6.D) at 8.30 P.M. R.M. Capt	
FINS	8		Sections supplied limbers & prepared to line.	
			Reconnoitred left eye line (200 mtg Dys)	
			Positions good.	
			Weather cloudy & showery. R.M. Capt	

WAR DIARY
or
INTELLIGENCE SUMMARY.
(Erase heading not required.)

Army Form C. 2118.

Place	Date	Hour	Summary of Events and Information	Remarks and references to Appendices
FINS	July 1917 9.		Nos I & IV Sections went into the line on R. sector and relieved 7 guns of 175 M.G. Coy. Just after relief shell pitched (burst) near a gun of No I Section. Gun was hit & 2 men (Pte Woolfan and Pte ____) badly wounded. Germans attempted a raid on the left. They did not succeed in entering our trenches but left 7 dead men on wire. Otherwise situation normal. RJM Capt	
	10		Nos II & III Sections went into the line on L. sector and relieved 8 guns of 200 M.G. Coy. Relief carried out successfully by H.Q. established in a whole house in METZ. Weather cloudy. RJM Capt	

Place	Date	Hour	Summary of Events and Information	Remarks and references to Appendices
METZ	1917 July 11		Visited Right Section. Guns in this sector are all in support line and can do no good at all. 2 guns moved. 1 placed near top of A.S.H & R. ALLEY. The other placed in front line facing FR doing own work. Situation quiet. R/M Capt	
	12		2 more guns of N.O.E. Section moved to front line. Nearly the whole front of R sector is now covered by our M.G's. The difficulty is there are at present no shelters at all in front line. I gather two have been constructed for guns in A.S.H & R ALLEY. Situation quiet. R/M Capt	

Army Form C. 2118.

WAR DIARY
INTELLIGENCE SUMMARY.
(Erase heading not required.)

Place	Date	Hour	Summary of Events and Information	Remarks and references to Appendices
MET Z	1917 July 13.		Accompanied an R.E. Tunnelling by officer round the R. sector. He is going to construct 2 deep dug outs in front line which Bng. Gen. wishes to be for M.G.s. The 2 dug outs are so sighted that 2 gunteams supas 1 and 3 gunteams the other. Situation quiet. RJM Capt.	
	14.		Visited BILLEM doctor (N°III section). Left gun in support line moved to front line by night. Withdrew to old position by day. Emplacements for this gun constantly shelter for other first line gun of this section completed. Situation normal. RJM Capt.	

WAR DIARY or INTELLIGENCE SUMMARY

Army Form C. 2118.

Place	Date	Hour	Summary of Events and Information	Remarks and references to Appendices
METZ EN COUTURE	July 15 1917		Visited R.S. Co. Everything OK. Have got slightly changed and an extra tng immediately of the 2 deep dug outs. Arranged for officers men of 5 + 11 Sects to take all off guns at EV Sect for 24 hours from 16-7-17 to allow EV Section 48 hours out of the line. R.M. Capt. Weather - wet at eng. after but a steady RM Capt.	
	16		Went with Lt FRICKER round the guns of 215 M.G.Coy which we take over on night 19-7-17. LT PALLISER obtained O.C. 206 M.G.Coy round all guns from R. boundary to QUEENS LANE. 40th Section moved to billets at METZ R.M.Capt Weather showery Situation normal	

WAR DIARY
INTELLIGENCE SUMMARY
(Erase heading not required.)

Army Form C. 2118.

Place	Date	Hour	Summary of Events and Information	Remarks and references to Appendices
METZ	1917 July 17		206 M.G. Coy relieved 11 guns of 198 M.G. Coy in the Bolo sector from Right Boundary to QUEENS LANE inclusive. Relief completed satisfactorily — N°s I and II Sections proceeded to Camps at Transport Lines. Situation quiet. RM Capt	
"	18		N° III section still in the line in BIXHEM FARM sector. The enemy shelled this sector more than usual during the day. Direct hits were obtained in SHERWOOD AVENUE C.T. and Support Line. No casualties. Situation otherwise quiet. RM Capt	

WAR DIARY
INTELLIGENCE SUMMARY

Army Form C. 2118.

Place	Date	Hour	Summary of Events and Information	Remarks and references to Appendices
METZ	July 19		No. IV Section (2nd Lieut. and Lt Laurie) relieved 1 section of 215 M.G. Coy in the trenches in neighbourhood of TRESCAULT village - priming carts out with 11 section in BILHEM sector. Relief completed satisfactorily. BILHEM sector by our shelled (more than usual) chiefly support line and C.T's. Situation otherwise normal. R.M. Capt.	
	20		During afternoon and evening enemy again shelled support line in BILHEM sector. A few 8" shells were used but mostly 5.9" and 4.2". One 8" shell pitched on parapet in the centre of shaft of a M.G. deep dug-out. The whole shaft collapsed & infantry who were sitting in the top were buried and killed.	

WAR DIARY
INTELLIGENCE SUMMARY

Army Form C. 2118.

Place	Date	Hour	Summary of Events and Information	Remarks and references to Appendices
METZ	1917 July 20 (continued)		Lt. H.S. LING, expecting the enemy to send after this bombardment, went to his front line guns and stayed there during following events to. At about 10.15 P.M. the enemy put down a heavy barrage on our front line on Bde on our left & and also on left half of our TRESCAULT sector. After about 5 minutes barrage lifted and changed to a box barrage. Lt Fricker & H. Laurie, who were waiting their guns, immediately made their way through part of the barrage to their left front line gun which was in the barrage. When he got to the trench Lt Fricker found no infantry in the trench except Interval Corp Johnson. He found his gun team under Corp Johnson, got their gun firing shots out to ..... The enemy raiding trenches on our left with 100 men. On his firing was taken back by them [None?] of our men	

WAR DIARY
INTELLIGENCE SUMMARY.
(Erase heading not required.)

Army Form C. 2118.

Place	Date	Hour	Summary of Events and Information	Remarks and references to Appendices
METZ (continued)	1917 July 20		were missing. Own casualties :— 4 killed 50 wounded. 1 German prisoner taken. Enemy casualties unknown. Casualties in this coy & Wing Coy.	R.M. Capt
-"-	21		No I Section relieved No III Section in BILLEM Sector. No II -"- -"- -"- -"- TRESCAULT -"- Both reliefs completed O.K. about 10.36 p.m. L/Cpl Reid, Sgt. Bateman and Pte Berry of No III Section were wounded. Lt Pollixen went up to No II Section for the night. Situation very quiet.	R.M. Capt
-"-	22		Lt Tucker returned to Pollixen. Situation quiet in both sectors. Weather fine and very hot.	R.M. Capt

WAR DIARY
INTELLIGENCE SUMMARY.
(Erase heading not required.)

Army Form C. 2118.

Place	Date	Hour	Summary of Events and Information	Remarks and references to Appendices
METZ	1917 July 23		Small raid carried out by 175 Inf Bde on our immediate left. 2 M.G.s of Lieut Stuckers fired up the valley towards HAVRINCOURT village. Raid successful. 2 wounded prisoners captured. Situation otherwise quiet. CMCapt	
	24		Day light position being constructed for No 7 gun. The gun team for this gun moved into the cellar of a house in TRESCAULT village. Situation quiet. PMCapt	

WAR DIARY or INTELLIGENCE SUMMARY

Army Form C. 2118.

(Erase heading not required.)

Place	Date	Hour	Summary of Events and Information	Remarks and references to Appendices
METZ	1917 25		Everything very quiet on both sectors. An enemy aeroplane frequently flies very low over No Man's Land in front of both sectors. Each section has 1 gun mounted by day for anti-aircraft firing. These guns have plenty of rotation. Situation very quiet. WM Capt.	
	26		Capt Hughes, O.C. 28 M.G. Coy. accompanied me round the whole sector to see all positions before taking over. We proposed had one gun mounted in shell hole facing support line near BIXHEM FARM enemy wire observed frequently walking along a road at TOMBOIS HARINCOURT. Guns fired a rate of 3000 to the objective & listened but enemy did not return fire. Very quiet. WM Capt.	

WAR DIARY
or
INTELLIGENCE SUMMARY
(Erase heading not required.)

Army Form C. 2118.

Place	Date	Hour	Summary of Events and Information	Remarks and references to Appendices
METZ	1916 July 27		Warning order received for company to move to SIRE NCOURT on or about July 31st 1917. Spent night on left sector had reinforced all guns. Situation quiet – enemy MG's rather active at night – sweeping along parapet. R.M.M Capt.	
	28		A new out post line is being constructed about 250+ in front of our present front line. A good belt of wire is already planted. Posts being constructed in loss of this are to be from these posts to a very good arty line of our enemy front line. Weather extremely warm. Situation quiet. R.M.M Capt.	

WAR DIARY / INTELLIGENCE SUMMARY

Army Form C. 2118.

Place	Date 1917	Hour	Summary of Events and Information	Remarks and references to Appendices
METZ	July 29		192 M.G. Coy relieved by 28 M.G. Coy in line. Relief completed by 6.0 P.M. – all gun teams relieved by daylight, the 6 sections came back to Coy H.Q. at METZ. Weather wet and dull. Situation quiet. R.D.M Capt.	
"	30		Company arrived into camp at NEUVILLE in tents. Men taken over from details of 28 M.G. Coy. Weather wet and showery. R.D.M Capt	
NEUVILLE	31		4 Platoon left camp for BAPAUME 5.30 A.M with 6 Limbers. Limber left camp and proceeded to BAPAUME by bus 9.30 A.M. Train left BAPAUME 2.0 P.M arrived BÉAUMETZ 5.30 P.M. Company arrived SIMENCOURT about 6.15 P.M. Men and some officers in huts remainder billeted in farm houses. Weather wet. R.D.M Capt	

Army Form C. 2118.

198 Machine Gun Coy

WAR DIARY
INTELLIGENCE SUMMARY
(Erase heading not required.)

Place	Date 1917	Hour	Summary of Events and Information	Remarks and references to Appendices
SIMENCOURT	Aug 1		Company spent whole day refitting equipment etc and also cleaning billets which were in a bad state. Weather - wet	
			Company cooking arranged to be carried out at 1 cookhouse only - not section cookhouses. R.M. Capt.	
"	2		Section Parades - gun drill - 1 hour Physical Training - just over ½ parade grounds - owing to state of weather the Limber field is nearly under water. R.M. Capt.	
"	3	6.30am	Saluting drill and guard mounting drill	
		9am	Firing stoppages on range - the range is severe by a stop butt but with care we can fire up to 100 yds. Instruction in indirect fire for M.Gs. R.M. Capt.	

Army Form C. 2118.

WAR DIARY
INTELLIGENCE SUMMARY.
(Erase heading not required.)

Instructions regarding War Diaries and Intelligence Summaries are contained in F. S. Regs., Part II. and the Staff Manual respectively. Title pages will be prepared in manuscript.

Place	Date	Hour	Summary of Events and Information	Remarks and references to Appendices
OMIECOURT	1917 Aug 4	5.30	Saluting and arms drill	
		9.0	1 Section firing on range. Remainder - gun drill - L.A. mechanism & breech P.T. Weather inclined to be wet. RDM Capt	
"	5	5.30 am	Company parade for Inspection march to Church Parade in parade ground of 18th London Regt. RDM Capt	
"	6	6.30 am	P.T. exercises	
		9.30 am	2 sections firing & stoppages. 2 — digging emplacements in chaeuvel trenches. Weather fairly dry. RDM Capt	

Army Form C. 2118.

WAR DIARY
INTELLIGENCE SUMMARY.
(Erase heading not required.)

Place	Date	Hour	Summary of Events and Information	Remarks and references to Appendices
SIMENCOURT	1917 Aug 7.	6.30AM	Sgt Majors parade.	
		9 AM	2 Sections firing stoppages on range. 2 — digging emplacements on old disused trenches. P.M Capt	
	8	5.30AM	Company paraded for Brigade Route March. Dress full marching order. 1st line Transport came with the company. Route — SIMENCOURT — BERNEVILLE — WANQUETIN and then to billets. 10 men fell out. Arrived back in billets about 8.45 am. Section parades 10 Am to 12.30 pm. Weather fine. P.M Capt	

WAR DIARY
INTELLIGENCE SUMMARY.
(Erase heading not required.)

Army Form C. 2118.

Place	Date	Hour	Summary of Events and Information	Remarks and references to Appendices
SPRIMOURT	1917 Aug 9		1st Brigade Inter Section M.G. Competition. (Bole Sports td)	
		2.30pm	Section Lecturing Paraded	
			Judged by Lieut M.G.O and O.C. 215 M.G. Coy	
			Results: 1st No III Section	
			2" - II -	
			3" - IV -	
			4" - I -	
			The four Nos III . II Sections enter for the final	
			Built to be judged by Brigadier	
			RM Capt.	
	10		1st Inf Brigade a'll round competition	
			1st round Bos. Football Competition	
			198 M.G.Coy 1 Coy of 16 Rd London Bgt	
			WON 2 - 0.	
			RM Capt.	

WAR DIARY
INTELLIGENCE SUMMARY
(Erase heading not required.)

Army Form C. 2118.

Place	Date	Hour	Summary of Events and Information	Remarks and references to Appendices
SIMENCOURT	1917 Aug 11	8.30 am	Company paraded for bathing at BERNEVILLE Baths	
		10.20	Section Parades	
			Weather fine	
			R/M Capt	
		12.11 AM	Bde drill Competition (Best platoon of each Batt — equivalent to a platoon from 2 sections of MG Coy) Judged by Brig. Gen H. Stockwell – 175 E/R Bde. Company came out last. Arms drill was very good – marching was poor	
		3.0 pm	2nd Round Football 192 MG Coy v Coy of 2/8 on Jordan Regt Result Lost 0-2 Very good game. R/M Capt	

WAR DIARY

INTELLIGENCE SUMMARY

Army Form C. 2118.

(Erase heading not required.)

Place	Date	Hour	Summary of Events and Information	Remarks and references to Appendices
SIMENCOURT	1917 Aug 13		Final of M.G. Company Competition. Nos II & III Sections fired at BERNEVILLE Range. Turnout judged by Brig. Gen Higgins Comdg 174 Inf Bde. M.G. Drill judged by Lieut M.G.O. and Bde Major. Result :— 1st No III Section 2nd " II " No III Section are thus the first holders of Challenge Cup presented to Company by the Brigade. R.M. Capt.	
	14		2 Sections digging emplacements and practising trenches with sandbags under R.E. instruction. Remainder firing in rapid and on range — stoppages firing with Rest Respirators on. R.M. Capt.	

WAR DIARY
INTELLIGENCE SUMMARY
(Erase heading not required.)

Army Form C. 2118.

Place	Date	Hour	Summary of Events and Information	Remarks and references to Appendices
CINEPACOURT	1917 Aug. 15		No 1, 2, & 4 Sections — section parades. No III Section parade for digging emplacements under R.E. Supervision. RM Capt.	
	16	7:00am	Company paraded for Bde Tactical scheme to take place in trenches at WAILLY. No guns were attached to Battalions. 4 guns were consolidated in 2nd and 3rd Objectives respectively. Pulled packs were of great assistance although very heavy. Weather — fine. RM Capt.	

WAR DIARY
INTELLIGENCE SUMMARY
(Erase heading not required.)

Army Form C. 2118.

Place	Date	Hour	Summary of Events and Information	Remarks and references to Appendices
SOMERCOURT	1917 Aug 17		Lectures paraded under their own officers for gym drill – map reading and lectures. In the picture march competition each section had to march 3 miles – proved to gym in time – fitness etc. Result No II certain won. The distance was not long enough for good test. R.M. Capt.	
	18	6.30 am	Squad drill	
		9.0	Lectures paraded – arachnoism – P.T. etc. R.M. Capt.	
			Wether fine	
	19		Church parade	
			Afternoon – Transport & H.Q. paraded to a photograph. Final – Bn v Bn – Football 48th Bn – 2 goals beat 45th Bn 1 goal R.M. Capt.	

Army Form C. 2118.

WAR DIARY
or
INTELLIGENCE SUMMARY.
(Erase heading not required.)

Place	Date	Hour	Summary of Events and Information	Remarks and references to Appendices
SIMENCOURT	1917 Aug 20		2 lectures – "formation in the attack". 2 lectures digging under R.E. supervision in old trenches at back of village. RMCapt	
—	21		Divisional Day at Wailly trenches. 174 Bde attacked German trenches – 175 Bde defended them. Criticism of MG work. Umpires were again very unsuccessful. Weather – showery. RMCapt	
—	22		1 lecture digging under R.E. supervision. Remainder acting couples – formation in the attack – gun drill & topography. Weather fine. RMCapt	

WAR DIARY
or
INTELLIGENCE SUMMARY.
(Erase heading not required.)

Army Form C. 2118.

Place	Date	Hour	Summary of Events and Information	Remarks and references to Appendices
SIMENCOURT	1917 Aug 23		Marching orders received to move to POPERINGHE area. Brigade Parade at BERNEVILLE - prior. given by the General - Lecture by Major. Courson - 3rd army Gymnastic staff on the "Spirit of the Bayonet". Packing off stores etc. Transport left Simencourt at midnight for ARRAS. R.M. Capt. Weather inclined to be wet.	
	24	1.0 am	Company left billets for No 9 station ARRAS. Entrained at ARRAS.	
		5.54 am	Departed ARRAS	
		1.45 pm	Arrived GODASWAEVELD (via S⁺ POL - MARLES). Detrained. Marched to billets at POPERINGHE. R.M. Capt.	

Army Form C. 2118.

WAR DIARY
or
INTELLIGENCE SUMMARY.
(Erase heading not required.)

Place	Date	Hour	Summary of Events and Information	Remarks and references to Appendices
POPERINGHE	Aug 25	10 AM	Complete inspection of whole company – kit – equipment – gas appliances etc. Inspecting leaders and cleaning gun equipment. RM Capt.	
—	26		2nd Lieut Smith – 2nd Lieut Ling (A.S.) and myself went by bus (with officers of 2/7 Bn) to ESSEX farm in order to Reconnoitred trenches and gained as much information as possible with a view to taking over that part of line. RM Capt. Weather showery.	
—	27		Rations franchised entrenching digging in accordance with pamphlet issued by M. Gen more. Guns overhauled and Made ready for the line. Weather cool – rain. RM Capt.	

Army Form C. 2118.

WAR DIARY
INTELLIGENCE SUMMARY.
(Erase heading not required.)

Instructions regarding War Diaries and Intelligence Summaries are contained in F. S. Regs., Part II. and the Staff Manual respectively. Title pages will be prepared in manuscript.

Place	Date	Hour	Summary of Events and Information	Remarks and references to Appendices
POPERINGHE	28		Gun Drill and lectures. Packing limbers and billets cleaned	
		5.0 PM	Deputation to have to SEIGERS CAMBERG Camp. Lieuts Bird and Long (M.B.) and 15 O.R. left at POPERINGHE no company orders. Weather improving. RM Capt	
REMMERS- BERG	29		No III and IV Sections went into the line and relieved 2 guns of 206 M.G. Coy Relief completed at 10 P.M. 4 guns in large concrete gallery called the BUND 3 guns in small concrete gallery called the crossways of the STEENEBECK 1 gun journey and MON DE HIBOU and 2 in TRIANGLE Farm. Weather showery - wind west. RM Capt	

Army Form C. 2118.

WAR DIARY
INTELLIGENCE SUMMARY.
(Erase heading not required.)

Instructions regarding War Diaries and Intelligence Summaries are contained in F. S. Regs., Part II. and the Staff Manual respectively. Title pages will be prepared in manuscript.

Place	Date	Hour	Summary of Events and Information	Remarks and references to Appendices
CANAL BANK	30		Visited guns in line with D.M.90 - started at 2.30 A.M. By the time we had crossed the STEENEBECK it had become too light to go further forward. All guns reached their positions safely last night. One shell pitched in canal immediately in front of dug out of No 6 at 9.0 A.m. Situation normal. Weather dull but no rain. Wind West. R M Capt	

Army Form C. 2118.

WAR DIARY
INTELLIGENCE SUMMARY.
(Erase heading not required.)

Place	Date	Hour	Summary of Events and Information	Remarks and references to Appendices
KSER CANAL BANK	1917 Aug 31.		Enemy put down heavy barrage round 2 MEBUS at m.m. D'HIBOU last night from 8.40 p.m. to 9.45 p.m. It then slackened but he still harassed the TEENEBECK at intervals throughout the night. Weather fair and sunny. Wind - West. JM Capt	

198 Machine Gun
Company
M.G.C.

War Diary

VOLUME X

No. 198
MACHINE GUN
COMPANY.
No.
Date 2/10/17

WAR DIARY
INTELLIGENCE SUMMARY.
(Erase heading not required.)

Army Form C. 2118.

Place	Date	Hour	Summary of Events and Information	Remarks and references to Appendices
YSER CANAL BANK	1917 Sept 1		Enemy put down rather heavier barrage than usual on STEENBEEK about 4.4.5 AM. Enemy artillery active round MON DU HIBOU until 8 oak am. Rest of day fairly quiet. 2 guns ranged from BUND and placed in mortar dugout near REGINA CROSS covering approaches to STEENBEEK. Position MK. Wind WEST - strong. Situation normal. RdM Capt.	
	2		2 guns fire from REGINA CROSS and on from the BUND. engaged HUBNER FARM and FLORA COTT and enemy ration tracks 6000 rounds fired. Everything quiet. Wind fresh - west. Situation normal. RdM Capt.	

WAR DIARY
INTELLIGENCE SUMMARY
(Erase heading not required.)

Army Form C. 2118.

Place	Date	Hour	Summary of Events and Information	Remarks and references to Appendices
CANAL BANK	1917 Sept 3		Enemy put down light barrage every fairly heavy shells on MON DU HIBOU from 8.30 pm to 9.15 pm. Our machine gunners let in back so he was entering the redins. He then lifted the barrage onto communications h ALBERTA using some teen gas & shells. After this all was quiet. Same targets engaged to yesterday – 6,000 rounds fired. Situation normal and very quiet. Old East RMM Capt	
	4		2 guns fired at same target as previously – 5000 rounds fired. Situation quiet. A.L. bombs were dropped on back areas – complete wind nil. RMM Capt.	

Army Form C. 2118.

WAR DIARY
INTELLIGENCE SUMMARY.
(Erase heading not required.)

Instructions regarding War Diaries and Intelligence Summaries are contained in F. S. Regs., Part II. and the Staff Manual respectively. Title pages will be prepared in manuscript.

Place	Date	Hour	Summary of Events and Information	Remarks and references to Appendices
CANAL BANK	Sept 1917 5		Situation normal. Usual intermittent shelling of STEENBEEK.	
			HUBNER Fm engaged during night — 400 rounds fired. RM Capt	
	6		No 1 section relieved No IV sect at MON DU HIBOU	
			" " III " " the BOND	
			2 Ptd slightly wounded during the relief. Situation quiet. RM Capt	
	7		2/6"B" carried out a reconn. raid on the PROMENADE	
			2/4 Peppered took one gun out to VANCOUVER Fm to cover the left flank. RM Capt	
			Situation otherwise normal	
	8		Both on left carried spot fire	
			Enemy often respect and shelled tracks during the night. RM Capt	
	9		Small raid carried out by infantry against enemy fortified shell holes. RM Capt	
			Situation quiet	

Army Form C. 2118.

WAR DIARY
or
INTELLIGENCE SUMMARY.
(Erase heading not required.)

Place	Date	Hour	Summary of Events and Information	Remarks and references to Appendices
	1917 Sept			
CANAL BANK	10		Enemy shelled MGN DU MIROI fairly heavily during the day and for 10 minute intervals during the night. Situation otherwise normal. R.M. Capt.	
"	11		Company relieved by 206 M.G. Coy. Relief completed at about 1.30 A.M. 12-9-17. Sections within relieved proceeded to REIGERSBURG Camp. Situation quiet except for heavy gasshelling round ADMIRALS Road. R.M. Capt.	
"	12		Company moved to camp at DAMBRE Camp in afternoon. Cleaning up etc all the morning. R.M. Capt.	
DAMBRE	13		All the attached infantry (64) detailed to sections for carrying party in attack which will take place in near future. R.M. Capt.	
"	14		Training of attached infantry on the gun. Sections practising advancing in attack formation. R.M. Capt.	

WAR DIARY
INTELLIGENCE SUMMARY
(Erase heading not required.)

Army Form C. 2118.

Instructions regarding War Diaries and Intelligence Summaries are contained in F. S. Regs., Part II. and the Staff Manual respectively. Title pages will be prepared in manuscript.

Place	Date 1917	Hour	Summary of Events and Information	Remarks and references to Appendices
DUNKIRK Camp	Sept 15		Brigade Field day at GUEMPS. Object to practise following attack. Brigade went on behind some battalions and to same objective as they went in Zero Day. Batteries were not attached to Battalions. Sixteen guns per section to go to definite objectives. They are to put down the infantry as possible F.A.'s bombed the dumps at the Chateau. Several cars hit — 3 drivers — 1 off + 3 sects — 7 infantry carrying party.	
	16		Lecture practising points brought out on yesterday's experiences.	
	17		Final inspection of equipment, ammunition etc. Setting machinery moving into action quietly in light countries — + getting ammunition quickly out of FORAGE Packs	

Army Form C. 2118.

WAR DIARY
or
INTELLIGENCE SUMMARY.
(Erase heading not required.)

Instructions regarding War Diaries and Intelligence Summaries are contained in F. S. Regs., Part II. and the Staff Manual respectively. Title pages will be prepared in manuscript.

Place	Date	Hour	Summary of Events and Information	Remarks and references to Appendices
DAMBAE (ACRE)	1917 Sept 12		Final Brigade practice of the attack. Everything went well. Divisional actions marched to Camp at REIGERSBURG (a.m.) Section (carried the packs) proceeded up the line at 6.30 PM to HUGEL HALLES. They then carried ammunition and water and formed a forward dump at Tank at VANCOUVER. RM Capt.	
	19		Sections left camp as follows:- No IV Section at 6.30 PM to MON DUTIBOO No I - 10 PM - enemy positions No II - 10 PM - Fired for 2 hours at 10 PM. Otherwise very quiet. RM Capt	

A6945 Wt. W1442/M1160 350,000 12/16 D.D. & L. Forms/C./2118/14.

Army Form C. 2118.

WAR DIARY
-or-
INTELLIGENCE SUMMARY.
(Erase heading not required.)

Instructions regarding War Diaries and Intelligence Summaries are contained in F. S. Regs., Part II. and the Staff Manual respectively. Title pages will be prepared in manuscript.

Place	Date	Hour	Summary of Events and Information	Remarks and references to Appendices
ALBERTA	Sept 1917 20	5.40 AM	Zero hour. Attack progressed very well. All given objectives except 1 of 7½ Regiment and 1 of Lieut Smiths both of which were hit. Toward dump at VANCOUVER proved most useful. Carrying Party was invaluable. RM Capt	
" "	21		Situation practically clear. All objectives taken except 1 group of methises [pillboxes?] afterwards silenced by 215 MG Coy. In evening Relieved [Revilling?] of operations is being made but is not yet completed. RM Capt	
REIGERSBURG	22		Company marching REIGERSBURG Camp cleaning up and resting. Lt FRICKER and Lt Ling WR wounded in circumstances. RM Capt	

Army Form C. 2118.

WAR DIARY
INTELLIGENCE SUMMARY.
(Erase heading not required.)

Instructions regarding War Diaries and Intelligence Summaries are contained in F.S. Regs., Part II. and the Staff Manual respectively. Title pages will be prepared in manuscript.

Place	Date	Hour	Summary of Events and Information	Remarks and references to Appendices
REINFASSER f CAMP	Sept 23 1917		Whole day spent in filling ammunition boxes, cleaning guns etc. Weather very fine. From fairly strong at night. RPM Capt.	
—	24		Preparing 10 gun teams to go into the line tomorrow to assist in MG Barrage for 175 Bde attack at dawn 25-9-17. The Divisional MG Coy (214 m.g.coy) only sending up 6 guns although we were in the attack on 20th and they were not. RPM Capt.	
—	25		6 guns under Lieuts: Reid & Ling (H.S.) proceeded to SPRINGFIELD and prepared for the barrage. 2 guns under Lieft Pepperall took over from 2gunsof 215 MG Coy at STROPPE Fm. 2 guns under Lieut: Pallies proceeded to HUBNER Fm for barrage work. Lieut: Pallies was in charge of all 10 guns. All guns got into position without casualties. RPM Capt.	

WAR DIARY
INTELLIGENCE SUMMARY

(Erase heading not required.)

Army Form C. 2118.

Place	Date	Hour	Summary of Events and Information	Remarks and references to Appendices
SPRINGFIELD CAMP	Sept 26 1917		Zero hour was 5.50 AM. Scenes at SPRINGFIELD managed to fire a few rounds before our barrage but seemed to forget to stop on the arrival of ours that they had to stop. These guns were withdrawn to camp that night by order of 175 Bde. R.M. Capt.	
	27		5 men killed & 3 wounded as result of our 10 guns going up & against in the barrage. Got lot of work done — M.L. Hun who was on place from which a M.G. barrage could be fired. R.M. Capt.	
	28		Cleaning up etc. Enemy aeroplane dropped a trifle over number of bombs in neighbourhood from 8.30 pm till about midnight. R.M. Capt.	

Army Form C. 2118.

WAR DIARY
INTELLIGENCE SUMMARY.
(Erase heading not required.)

Instructions regarding War Diaries and Intelligence Summaries are contained in F. S. Regs., Part II. and the Staff Manual respectively. Title pages will be prepared in manuscript.

Place	Date	Hour	Summary of Events and Information	Remarks and references to Appendices
PEPPERSBURG CAMP	1917 Sept 29		Preparing for move to CHERQUES (new rest area). All camp severely bombed from 8 pm till 2.0 AM. Many casualties occurred in horse lines. No casualties in the company. RMM Capt.	
	30		Move of personnel postponed till 1-10-17. Transport moved off at 7.30 AM and proceeded to WORMHOUDT and POPERINGHE arriving at 5.30 pm. Excellent camping ground for mules, limbers and men. Weather very fine. Many bombs were heard in direction of POPERINGHE. RMM Capt.	

1577 Wt.W10791/1773 500,000 1/15 D. D. & L. A.D.S.S./Forms/C. 2118.

198th Coy.

M G C

War Diary
A.F. C 2118

Volume XI

October 1917

Army Form C. 2118.

WAR DIARY
INTELLIGENCE SUMMARY.
(Erase heading not required.)

Instructions regarding War Diaries and Intelligence Summaries are contained in F. S. Regs., Part II. and the Staff Manual respectively. Title pages will be prepared in manuscript.

Place	Date 1917	Hour	Summary of Events and Information	Remarks and references to Appendices
REKSBORG CAMP	Oct. 1		Company left camp at 1.20 p.m. for VLAMERTINGHE station. Train supposed to leave at 4.20 p.m. A train was made up at POPERINGHE and out along. Actually left VLAMERTINGHE about 10 p.m. train ?topped many times on journey owing to bombs being dropped at various places. ?Transport continued their march — left WORMHOUDT at 7 a.m. and arrived CLERQUES at 5.20 p.m. Weather very fine. R?M Capt.	
CLERGUES	2		Company detrained at AUDRUICQ about 4.0 a.m. and marched CLERQUES at 8.0 a.m. By march route at 8.0 a.m. Day spent in sleeping and cleaning up. Weather still very fine. R?M Capt.	
—	3		Section Parades — unloading limbers, stores and gun equipment. Cleaning guns etc. R?M Capt. Weather very fine.	
—	4		Section Parades — gun drill — mechanism — P.T. Site for range for stoppages discovered at foot of hill north of village. R?M Capt. Weather — showery and very windy	

WAR DIARY
INTELLIGENCE SUMMARY

Army Form C. 2118.

Place	Date	Hour	Summary of Events and Information	Remarks and references to Appendices
CIERQUES	1917 OCT. 5	8.30am	Company under Sgt. Major for lecturing, drill and rifle exercises. Large pn. pn. of company now consists of new drafts. These are good men but then discipline is rather slack but is improving under supervision.	
			Section parade - gun drill - mechanism etc - too wet for firing. Weather wet in morning - fine in afternoon.	
		10am	20 men proceeded to CALAIS by motor lorry under Role arrangements for the day. Weather wet in morning. Raining all morning. Weather too wet for any outdoor work. Parades in Skillets - Lectures - mechanism etc. RDM Capt	
	6			
	7	8.30	Company paraded for Church service on ground of 217th Bn London Regt. Weather fine during morning - rained during afternoon. RDM Capt	
	8		2 sections had a toppees - all their new stuff men to take to the subjects they knew then second half seemed very much out of practice. Weather fine during morning - wet afternoon + evening. RDM Capt	

Army Form C. 2118.

WAR DIARY
INTELLIGENCE SUMMARY.
(Erase heading not required.)

Instructions regarding War Diaries and Intelligence Summaries are contained in F. S. Regs., Part II. and the Staff Manual respectively. Title pages will be prepared in manuscript.

Place	Date	Hour	Summary of Events and Information	Remarks and references to Appendices
GUERRUES	1917 9		Weather dry - men met for firing on range. Position billets. Nocturnes etc. RMCapt	
"	10		2 Lectures field stoppages on short range at quarry - went for tactical march - map reading - choice of M.G. positions. Weather dull - met not. RMCapt	
"	11		Same as for yesterday - sections doing apparatus work. Weather fine. RMCapt	
"	12		Misty rain all morning - work in billets - mechanism etc. RMCapt	
"	13		Brigade Route march. Each unit marched to LIGUES via BODENFORT and then returned to billets. Weather - wet misty rain whole day. RMCapt	

Army Form C. 2118.

WAR DIARY
INTELLIGENCE SUMMARY.
(Erase heading not required.)

Place	Date 1917	Hour	Summary of Events and Information	Remarks and references to Appendices
CHERQUES	Oct. 14	9 AM 9.30	Company paraded for Church Parade on ground of 2/7 Bn London Regt. Weather fine in morning - showery in evening. R&M/Capt	
"	15		2 Sections fired on short range. Work in billets - Lectures - etc. Tactical march - church of M.G. positions - map reading - enemy's range code - Whether showery. R&M/Capt	
"	16		No 3 & 4 Sections fired - application and traversing on 30+ range. No 1 & 2 Lectures practicing - attack formation - giving orders N.C.O.s and No 1 & 2 on the gun experiments to for changing from teams in to cases of casualties accordingly. Weather fine. R&M/Capt	

Army Form C. 2118.

WAR DIARY
or
INTELLIGENCE SUMMARY.
(Erase heading not required.)

Place	Date	Hour	Summary of Events and Information	Remarks and references to Appendices
VERQUES	17 Oct 1917		Nos 1-3 Sections firing stoppages with Best Reporters on No 2 Section - Gas drill - choosing M.G. Positions on range and around ground. Weather fine. RtM Capt.	
"	18	8.30	No 1 Section took the returns with them and went out for the day - carried out a Tactical Scheme. Remainder firing stoppages with textured answer and Bayo roads - map reading lectures	
		3.P.M	Demonstration in the afternoon of use of Message Rockets. Weather fine. RtM Capt.	

Army Form C. 2118.

WAR DIARY
INTELLIGENCE SUMMARY.
(Erase heading not required.)

Instructions regarding War Diaries and Intelligence Summaries are contained in F. S. Regs., Part II. and the Staff Manual respectively. Title pages will be prepared in manuscript.

Place	Date	Hour	Summary of Events and Information	Remarks and references to Appendices
CLERQUES	1917 Oct. 19		Transport moved off at 7 am on last days march to the forward area – fighting trains renewed behind 10th company. All sections fired 3 - 5 filled belts with gun ammunition. Weather fine. R.M.Cabot Capt.	
		2.50 pm	Company left HERQUESNEST 6.0 pm for station at AUDRUIC. Weather fine. R.M.Cabot Capt.	
POPERINGHE	21	12.5 am	Train detrained AUDRUIC 8. From POPERINGHE about 6.0 AM. Officers & N.M. Stores in some billets as last time – men in horse-drawn transport. Men's billets very dirty. R.M.Cabot	

Army Form C. 2118.

Army Form C. 2118.

WAR DIARY
INTELLIGENCE SUMMARY.
(Erase heading not required.)

Instructions regarding War Diaries and Intelligence Summaries are contained in F. S. Regs., Part II. and the Staff Manual respectively. Title pages will be prepared in manuscript.

Place	Date	Hour	Summary of Events and Information	Remarks and references to Appendices
POPERINGHE	1917 OCT. 22		16 men per battalion attached to M.G. Coy as ammunition carriers. these men being trained in the grounds that they can give a hand on the guns in case of emergency. Weather wet. 2/Lt F.G. SMITH left the company for instructor job in AMERICA. R.M. Capt.	
—	23		Company moved into new billets (?) - occupied huts - an old prisoner of war camp. Weather fine. R.M. Capt.	
—	24		Company moved up to SEIGE CAMP at 6.20 pm in huts - all the company together. Weather fine - raining evening. R.M. Capt.	

Army Form C. 2118.

WAR DIARY
INTELLIGENCE SUMMARY.
(Erase heading not required.)

Instructions regarding War Diaries and Intelligence Summaries are contained in F. S. Regs., Part II. and the Staff Manual respectively. Title pages will be prepared in manuscript.

Place	Date	Hour	Summary of Events and Information	Remarks and references to Appendices
SERRE (App)	1917 Oct 25		Orders received last night detailing B yum of 214 & 2 of 197 M G Coys to put down a barrage to attack by 173 — Recn.morning of 26th. No time for reconnoitring the ground. Positions for firing detailed just in rear of POELCAPPELLE. Zero hrs all got ditched on St JULIEN — POELCAPPELLE Rd. Practice detail to use wireless and impossible. Unable to obtain new positions. Capture had to be abandoned. Bn the line. R.M Capt.	
	26.		Attack of 173 — Bde much hindered by rain — It and was terrible. O C Coy at VARNA Fm (Rde H.Q.) to control barrage but was completely out of touch. Weather — very bad rain. R.M Capt.	

Army Form C. 2118.

WAR DIARY
or
INTELLIGENCE SUMMARY.
(Erase heading not required.)

Instructions regarding War Diaries and Intelligence Summaries are contained in F. S. Regs., Part II. and the Staff Manual respectively. Title pages will be prepared in manuscript.

Place	Date	Hour	Summary of Events and Information	Remarks and references to Appendices
SIEGE Camp	1917 Dec 2		Capt. R.S.G. MAYNE proceeded to U.K. with orders to report to the Tower, London - H.A.C. depot. From thence he would proceed to the United States of America as machine gun instructor to the U.S. Army. LIEUT. J.S. PALLISER was appointed C.O. vice Capt. Mayne. Nos 3 & 4 Sections proceeded to the line by bus. Guides were met from 214 Machine Gun Company & relief carried out on night 27/28th. Coys of the two Sections were disposed in front of OOSTCAPPELLE village in three concreted strong points viz - HELLES house - (3 guns) TRUCKS Fm (6 guns) Coulbery Rd at Smith near LOO CHAPELLE. During the night large numbers of the 173 Infantry were discovered to be completely exhausted & roamed strayed from their units. Every effort was made by the men of this unit to help them - water & food were given to them & rightly so, men were collected and sent back next morning. The conditions on the line made it almost impossible to serve the wounded. The road going up to the mene Bross, Duckboard tracks were undergoing to to the work. H.Shew M.	

Army Form C. 2118.

WAR DIARY
or
INTELLIGENCE SUMMARY.
(Erase heading not required.)

Place	Date	Hour	Summary of Events and Information	Remarks and references to Appendices
In the line at ROEUX	1917			
	Oct 28		An uneventful day in the line. Companies HQ moved to Brigade HQ at VITRHA Farm. Preparations for Brigade attack on the 30 inst. Nos 1 and 2 Sections moved to KEMPTON PARK CAMP - 3 cycles from the line. Communications in present sector extremely bad - Roads are bad in forward areas and dumps are too far away. Line ...	
	Oct 29		Orders received for Brigade attack at dawn of 30th. Objectives - Line of Farms round NEGUS corner 600 x & ... of Present Pos. Machine gun Barrage 80 guns arranged in two stand back during attack. 4 Guns moved up into the line to consolidate under command of Front & 2nd Suffolks, Infantry having proved to be 44th to attain same. No R.G.C. Brigade guns asked for. These guns to remain in position here unto so to proceed to objectives MORAY the said Park Farm were consolidated with the two	J. Potter Lt.

WAR DIARY
or
INTELLIGENCE SUMMARY.
(Erase heading not required.)

Army Form C. 2118.

Place	Date	Hour	Summary of Events and Information	Remarks and references to Appendices
In the line	Oct 1917		At dawn the 8th Royl London R. on the right & one Company of the 6th Bn	
Potijze	30		London R. attacked on Brigade front. Troops formed up on tapes without incident. At zero hour went forward to the attack but owing to the impossible state of the ground was unable to reach objectives with exception of Crater of the 6th London Regt. who attacked on Tigers Ground captured HUSHES Farm GALLIPOLI MEBUS. Four guns had to altogether stock fast throughout the attack & when it was ascertained that they were not required arrangements were made by Nov 1st for sections to relieve 37th sections in the original positions the same night. Four guns at HERLES Farm were knocked out by shell fire during the attack. These were replaced on relief. Relief completed at 11.p.m. Casualties 6 O.R.s	

H. Wilson M.

Army Form C. 2118.

WAR DIARY
or
INTELLIGENCE SUMMARY.
(Erase heading not required.)

Instructions regarding War Diaries and Intelligence Summaries are contained in F. S. Regs., Part II. and the Staff Manual respectively. Title pages will be prepared in manuscript.

Place	Date	Hour	Summary of Events and Information	Remarks and references to Appendices
Potijze Sect.	1917 Feb		Usual Coy duty in the line.	
P.S.E. Cat Nook	3/st		Efforts made by every section to collect everything in front of trenches, & numbers of wounded men were brought in to various posts.	
			Guides met relief companies of 2 sections of 2/5 W.Y. Regt at 3 PM at Bde HQ.	
			Company Hd moved to PHEASANT Farm. Relief completed by 9 P.M. Company handed to O.C 2/5 W.Y Regt 10 P.M.	
			Company withdrew to Kempton Park Camp for relief. Total Casualties Other (Other 27. 7 Machine Gunners probably)	
			12 Infantry Officers. Through the fact that every precaution was taken in care of wounded no cases of Trench feet were reported, although there were 3 days the line in mud. Trench Emergency was ordered to test her feet with whale oil for half an hour before going into the line. A change of socks was supplied in coming out.	
				Stollard ??

CONFIDENTIAL

WAR DIARY.

of

198th COMPANY

MACHINE GUN CORPS

From November 1st 1917 to December 1st 1917

Volume X

WAR DIARY
or
INTELLIGENCE SUMMARY.
(Erase heading not required.)

Army Form C. 2118.

Place	Date	Hour	Summary of Events and Information	Remarks and references to Appendices
SIEGE CAMP.	1917 Nov. 1st		Company moved from Renfrew Park Camp overnight to Siege Camp 1 mile south of EVERDINGHE. The Engineers spent in cleaning up the Camp. Everything was in Hut. Full inspections after inspection was made at 3 p.m. Attention to Personal Kit & Equipment made good. Lt. C.S. GAMON 4th CHESHIRE Regt. AND M.G.C. appointed Company 2nd in Command vice Lt. J.S. PALLISER. 3rd & 4th Postn. noted.	
	2nd		C.S.M. Parade at 7 A.M. — Sunday drill inaugurated. 9 AM Company parade. Gas and equipment thoroughly inspected & deficiencies supplied for. Lewis gun picketeds everything dumped up by 12 A.M.	
	3rd	9AM	2nd Lieut. Howell ordered immediately by Route March — distance 10 or 12 miles. Arrived in Camp at 1 P.M. Roads full of Traffic and marching extremely difficult. Foot inspection & general Turnout at 3 P.M.	

WAR DIARY
or
INTELLIGENCE SUMMARY.
(Erase heading not required.)

Army Form C. 2118.

Place	Date	Hour	Summary of Events and Information	Remarks and references to Appendices
Siege Camp	1917 Nov. 4		No training this day Sunday	
		10 AM	Inspection of Camp and huts by C.O.	
		11 AM	Company paraded under orderly officers for Baths. Afternoon — Football games.	Wallace K.
	5	7 AM	A.M. parade — M.O's squads etc.	
		9 AM	Section parades in Camp — Gun Drill, I.A etc. weather which for a week has been fine shews signs of breaking up.	Wallace K.
	6	7 AM	A.M. parade — M.O's squads at	
		9 AM	Section parades — squad drill	
		11 AM	B.G.C. 174 Bde addressed all Section officers together with Infantry officers in which he thanked them for the good work done in the Mot. — this action on the part of the B.G.C urges very much appreciated by officers of this unit.	
		11 AM to 1 PM	Route March by Sections distance 8 miles	Wallace K.

Army Form C. 2118.

WAR DIARY
or
INTELLIGENCE SUMMARY.
(Erase heading not required.)

Instructions regarding War Diaries and Intelligence Summaries are contained in F. S. Regs., Part II. and the Staff Manual respectively. Title pages will be prepared in manuscript.

Place	Date	Hour	Summary of Events and Information	Remarks and references to Appendices
Seaford Camp	1917 Mar			
	7th	7AM	C.M's Parade — squad drill — discipline etc	
	7th	9AM	Company Parade — full marching order inspection	
		9:30	Section Parades.	
		AM	Gun Drill etc	
		to	Gas drill combined with gun drill	
			No. 1 Running drill.	M.Auer Capt.
	8th	7AM	C.M's Parade — NCO's squads — discipline etc	Mather Capt
		9AM	Sections parade full marching order for Route march — distance 10 Miles	
		2PM	Kit & foot inspections. All anti-Gas appliances & clothes correct. M.Auer Capt	
	9th	9AM	Nos 1 & 2 Sections Parade under Section Officers.	
		10AM	Nos 3 & 4 Sections march to Kempton Park Camp to relieve 2 Sections of the 215th T.M.G Coy in Brigade reserve. Relief N.P. at 3PM. These two Sections prepare to proceed to the line the following day. J Mather Capt

Army Form C. 2118.

WAR DIARY
or
INTELLIGENCE SUMMARY.
(Erase heading not required.)

Instructions regarding War Diaries and Intelligence Summaries are contained in F. S. Regs., Part II. and the Staff Manual respectively. Title pages will be prepared in manuscript.

Place	Date	Hour	Summary of Events and Information	Remarks and references to Appendices
KEMPTON PARK.	1917 Nov 10th	3 AM	Nos 1 & 2 Sections relieve Nos 3 & 4 Sections at KEMPTON PARK. Nos 3 & 4 Sections proceed to the line and take over from 2/5 M.G. Coy. Disposition of Guns as follows:- 6 Guns in forward posts Disposition of Guns as follows:- 2 Guns in support. Guns & the Company cover the whole front held by the 174th Bde. The Front covered by the Bde lies due east of POELCAPPELLE and is 1200 yds in length. Ground is very bad in front of positions being very wet and swampy. Relief completed by 6 AM on the 10th. Reg. Ptl reced Kempton Pk. Casualties killed 1 O.R.	
	11th		Uneventful day in the line. Enemy attempted on our front is purely defensive. Very little shelling. Enemy artillery active on Artillery areas. Casualties killed 1 O.R. wounded 3 ORs.	H. Her Capt. Helher Capt.

Army Form C. 2118.

WAR DIARY
or
INTELLIGENCE SUMMARY.
(Erase heading not required.)

Instructions regarding War Diaries and Intelligence Summaries are contained in F.S. Regs., Part II. and the Staff Manual respectively. Title pages will be prepared in manuscript.

Place	Date	Hour	Summary of Events and Information	Remarks and references to Appendices
In the Line	1917 Sept.	—	Very quiet day in the line.	
POELCAPELLE D.			Two days rations and water sent up to Sections in the line. Roads in back areas very bad for transport therefore ration and water have to be carried considerable distance. Route taken duckboard tracks. No horses. E.A very active over forward positions. Engaged by every M.G. in support gun subsequently possible. Casualties Nil.	
	13	3pm	Nos 1 and 2 Sections leave Keyston Park to proceed to relieve Nos 3 & 4 Sections. Situation quiet during relief. Relief completed by 7 p.m. Each man carried 2 days rations and 2 days water. Casualties wounded 2 O.R's.	
	14		Nothing of importance occurred in the front. Casualties "Nil". Each man in the line carries whole oil tubes & oils.	

WAR DIARY
or
INTELLIGENCE SUMMARY.

Army Form C. 2118.

Place	Date	Hour	Summary of Events and Information	Remarks and references to Appendices
In the line nr. PT. CAPPELLE	1917 15.	3pm	Nos 3 & 7th Sections at KEMPTON Pk relieved by two Sections of 106 Machine Gun Coy. On relief these two sections withdraw to Siege Camp. Sections bathe in the afternoon and change clothes. Only days rations sent up to sections in the line. Orders received for Brigade relief on night 16/17th. Casualties. Nil. Sections at Siege Camp prepare hack Limbers etc ready for move.	
	16	2pm	Company Hdqrs of 106 M.G. Coy reconnoitres the line in the morning. Two Sections of 106 M.G. Coy at Kempton Pk proceed to the line relieve Nos 1 & 2 sections. Situation quiet during relief - relief complete by 6 pm. Sections withdraw to Kempton Pk & two from there to Siege Camp. Change of clothes & baths on arrival. H. Milner Capt.	

Army Form C. 2118.

WAR DIARY
or
INTELLIGENCE SUMMARY.
(Erase heading not required.)

Instructions regarding War Diaries and Intelligence Summaries are contained in F. S. Regs., Part II. and the Staff Manual respectively. Title pages will be prepared in manuscript.

Place	Date	Hour	Summary of Events and Information	Remarks and references to Appendices
Seaford Camp	1917			
	Nov 2/17	7am	Transport paraded. Coys left camp & marched to HERZEELE.	
		2/pm	Company parade. Moved to EVERDINGHE Sta. ventrain.	
	17		to HERZEELE.	
		3pm	Arrival of transport & destructors	
		5pm	Company.	
			Company occupies in camp. Accommodation is good. Provisions without standings in this area.	[signature] Capt.
HERZEELE 18			Sunday – Church parade at 10.30. The chimney on the dry – Men have a thorough wash & sprinkle Capt.	[signature] Capt.
	19	9am	First parade – No company parades by order of C.O. O Turnor.	
			All arms & equipment landers thoroughly overhauled, cleaned.	
		2 pm	Football Match. OFFICERS v Coy team. Result coy won 2 – 0. [signature]	[signature] Capt.

Army Form C. 2118.

WAR DIARY
or
INTELLIGENCE SUMMARY.
(Erase heading not required.)

Instructions regarding War Diaries and Intelligence Summaries are contained in F.S. Regs., Part II. and the Staff Manual respectively. Title pages will be prepared in manuscript.

Place	Date	Hour	Summary of Events and Information	Remarks and references to Appendices
HERZEELE	1917			
	19th Aug 1917		Full marching order parade.	
	20.	9:30.	2:00 a parade under OC Sections under Section officers - PT running drill.	
		10.30 to 11AM	Gun drill Squad drill General Gallery of discipling throughout } Selling drill throughout Evening	Witheroft
	21	9 AM	Sections Inspected for PT Running drill 9:00 a parade under OC	
		10.30 AM	Gun drill - IA - Stripping etc 2:00 a parade under Section Officers	
		12		
		5 PM	Voluntary drill.	
		2 PM	Foot ball. No 2 Section beat No 3 Section. 1 - 0. (Witness Toffe	

Army Form C. 2118.

WAR DIARY
or
INTELLIGENCE SUMMARY.
(Erase heading not required.)

Instructions regarding War Diaries and Intelligence Summaries are contained in F. S. Regs., Part II, and the Staff Manual respectively. Title pages will be prepared in manuscript.

Place	Date	Hour	Summary of Events and Information	Remarks and references to Appendices
EZEELE	22nd	9am	Route march 21st inst.	
		3pm	Rugby match. Company v 176th Bn hockey R. Captn won 11-8.	
			W. Hurd Captn	
	23rd	4pm	Route March – Full Marching order. EZEELE – WORMHOUDT – WILDER – BILLETS	
			W. Hurd Captn	
	24th	7am	Section inspected full order, full inspection. 4.30pm Lecture on musketry under Lother Lucas – Lt Wynne-Bell. Lecture C.S.M. Practice under C.S.M.	
			W. Hurd Captn	
		11am		
PROVEN	25-	9.30am	Company handed over transport to move to PROVEN (Map Ref. HAZEBROUCK). Bus A" Belgium (PROVEN). March by road taking over from 206th MG Coy at PLAISTOW CAMP. Men were billeted in barns.	

D. P. & L., London, E.C. (A-68J) Wt. W80J/M1672 320,000 4/17 Forms/C/2118/14 Sch. 52a

Army Form C. 2118.

WAR DIARY
or
INTELLIGENCE SUMMARY.
(Erase heading not required.)

Instructions regarding War Diaries and Intelligence Summaries are contained in F. S. Regs., Part II. and the Staff Manual respectively. Title pages will be prepared in manuscript.

Place	Date	Hour	Summary of Events and Information	Remarks and references to Appendices
PROVEN HERZEELE	25th	9.30 AM	Company Transport move from HERZEELE to St. MOMELIN (Map ref Belgium 1:100,000 HAZEBROUCK SA D 3) by road. Personnel billeted at St MOMELIN in barns. Animals in closed sheds.	
			Copies of Move Orders No 2 & No 3 attached.	A1
			Capt PALLISER J.S. & 3395 Pte HORROCKS E. proceeded to U.K on leave.	
			#47322 A/Sgt WAKELY proceeds to Base Camiers for the purpose of proceeding to UK to undergo a special NCOs course at GRANTHAM [Authority A.G A/30(0.1) dated 22.9.17] & is struck off the strength of the Company accordingly.	
			(S. Gannon Lieut)	
AFFRINGUES	26th	10 am	Company less Transport move by train from PROVEN, entraining at 11 am and detraining at WIZERNES (Map ref Belgium 1:100,000 HAZEBROUCK S.A C.A.) and by road marching to AFFRINGUES. (Map ref Belgium 1:100,000 HAZEBROUCK S.A A4) Company Transport moved from St. MOMELIN to AFFRINGUES joining Company at AFFRINGUES. Company billeted in old Chateau, animals in yard of Chateau, officers in village.	
			(S. Gannon Lieut)	

Army Form C. 2118.

WAR DIARY

INTELLIGENCE SUMMARY.

(Erase heading not required.)

Instructions regarding War Diaries and Intelligence Summaries are contained in F. S. Regs., Part II. and the Staff Manual respectively. Title pages will be prepared in manuscript.

Place	Date	Hour	Summary of Events and Information	Remarks and references to Appendices
WATTERDAL	27th	10.30am	Company (complete) march from AFFRINGUES to WATTERDAL (Nr prof Belgium) via ECQUES, HAZEBROUCK SA A4.) Company billeted in village. Officers & Sergeants in houses, OR in barns, animals in stables & sheds.	
			1 OR to Hospital as a struck off the strength	
				C.S. Gamon Lieut
WATTERDAL	28th	9am-1pm	Company Training	
		9 am	Coy Parade. Drill Order.	
		9.15-11.30	Cleaning of Gun Equipment, limbers etc	
		11.30	Inspection " " by Section Officers	
		12-1 pm	General Fatigues —	
			Lieut R A PEPPERAL M.C. admitted to Hospital.	
				C.S. Gamon Lieut
WATTERDAL	29th	9 am	Company Parade Drill Order	
		9.15-11 am	Section Parades. Gun drill S.A. & Rougher Drill NCOs under C.S.M. Range takers under A/Cpl Davies. Two runners per	

WAR DIARY
or
INTELLIGENCE SUMMARY.
(Erase heading not required.)

Army Form C. 2118.

Place	Date	Hour	Summary of Events and Information	Remarks and references to Appendices
	29th	11-12	Section under Lieut KING	
		12-1 pm	PT & Running	
			Squad Drill Short lecture 'Discipline'	
			C.S. Gawen Lieut	
	30th	9.0	Company Parade Drill Order	
		9.15-10.15	PT & Running	
		10.15-11.15	Gas Drill ½ hr P##Reduct, ½ hour Box Resp.	
		11.15-12 pm	Practical Fire Direction	
			2 O.R. reinforcements reported & were taken on strength	
			C.S. Gawen Lieut	

Appendix I

198 Machine Gun Company.
Order No II
Movement Orders by
Capt J.S. Palliser Commanding
198 M.G. Company. M.G.C.

24/11/17.

1. MOVE.
The Company will move from Herzeele to Watterdal as follows:-
NOV: 25. Herzeele - Proven - taking over from 206 M.G. Coy at Plaistow (F.9a.2.9. Sheet 27) by road.
NOV: 26. Proven to Area "A" by train - detraining at Woyerines.
NOV: 27. Area "A" to Area "B" to Watterdal.

2. Advance Party. 2Lt Trent - Sergeant Korrington and Pte Stevens will act as Advance Party - reporting to Lt Harrison-Jones outside School Herzeele at 7AM.

3. Guides - 1 Guide will report at Brigade Head Quarters at 7A.M. where he will meet a Lorry and direct same to Camp to pick up Camp Kettles etc.

4. Parade.
The Company will parade at 9.30 AM. and will pass the starting point (D.10.d.15) at 10 AM. following Brigade Head Quarters.

5. Dress - The Company will parade in full marching order - 1 Blanket being carried on the person

(2) Advance Party.
 Sergeant Bunn will act as advance party. This N.C.O. will be with a bicycle outside Schools at Herzeele at 6.15 A.M.

(3) Parade.
 This party (para 1) will parade under orders of the Transport Officer.
 Transport will be drawn up facing West ready to move off at 10.25 A.M. Head of Column 200 yards west of cross roads C.12.d.9.1 Sheet 27. Order of March 6th - 2/2nd H C F A - 5th - 7th 8th 198 M.G. Coy - 214 M.G. Coy.

(4) Dress.
 As per Para 5 Order no 2.

(5) Rations & Fodder.
 2 days rations and fodder will be carried under the orders of Transport Officer.

C. S. Gamon Lieut
for
CAPTAIN,
O.C. 198th M. G. COY.

24/11/17.

CONFIDENTIAL.

War Diary

of

198th Company

Machine Gun Corps

from December 1st 1917 to January 1st 1918

Volume XIII (Original)

Army Form C. 2118.

WAR DIARY
or
INTELLIGENCE SUMMARY.
(Erase heading not required.)

Place	Date	Hour	Summary of Events and Information	Remarks and references to Appendices
WATTERDAL	Dec 1st 1917	9 am	Company Parade Drill Order	
		9.15-10.15	Physical Training and Running. N.C.Os under C.S.M.	
		9.15 - 11 am	Range fatigues & Runners under Lieut. King	
		10.15-11 am	Lecture & Practical "Anti-Aircraft Work"	
		11.15-1 pm	Coy Parade under S.M. Drill Order.	
			13420. Sgt Nixon C.H. proceeds to NEUF.CHATEL on Veterinary Course.	
			1 O.R Reinforcement reported - is taken on the strength.	
			C.S.Gamon Lieut	
	2nd	10 am	Inspection of Rifles. — Coy baths during the day.	
			12812 Cpl CORBETT & 110824 S Pte COOPER rejoined the Company	
			C.S.Gamon Lieut	
	3rd	9.10 am to 2.pm	Firing on Range. 25 yards - Chiefly Stoppages	
			Each Section does one hours Physical Training during the day	
			C.S.Gamon Lieut	

Army Form C. 2118.

WAR DIARY
or
INTELLIGENCE SUMMARY.
(Erase heading not required.)

Instructions regarding War Diaries and Intelligence Summaries are contained in F. S. Regs., Part II. and the Staff Manual respectively. Title pages will be prepared in manuscript.

Place	Date	Hour	Summary of Events and Information	Remarks and references to Appendices
WATTERDAL	4th	9 am	Company Parade, Drill Order	
		9.15-10.15	Physical Training & Running	
		10.15-1pm	Section Training under Section Officers	
			1 OR admitted to hospital	
			C.S.Gamon Lt.	
	5th	9am-2pm	Firing on Range. Field firing.	
			C.S.Gamon Lt.	
	6th	9 am	Company Parade Drill Order.	
		9.15-10.15	Physical Training	
		10.15-11.15	Gun Drill, S.A, etc	
		11.15-12.15	Cleaning of MG Equipment	
		12.15-1pm	Lecture ("Barrage Fire")	
			# Company Sing Song in Evening	
			Coy. Transport less two limbers move to LUMBRES by Road.	
			C.S.Gamon Lt.	

Army Form C. 2118.

WAR DIARY
or
INTELLIGENCE SUMMARY.
(Erase heading not required.)

Instructions regarding War Diaries and Intelligence Summaries are contained in F. S. Regs., Part II. and the Staff Manual respectively. Title pages will be prepared in manuscript.

Place	Date	Hour	Summary of Events and Information	Remarks and references to Appendices
AFFRINGUES	7th	9.15am	Company less Transport(less two mules) & march by road from WATTERDAL to AFFRINGUES. Move orders attached. Company Transport move from KUMBRES to St MOMELIN by road. 55647 Cpl NUNN proceeds to CAMIERS on Course. R.C.S. Gower Lt	Appendix I
BROWN CAMP or POPERINGHE- ELVERDINGHE Road	8th	3 am	Company less Transport march to WIZERNE. Entraining at WIZERNE and then by train detraining at ELVERDINGHE and march to Brown Camp (Map Ref Belgium Sheet 28 N.W. A 23 b 20.60.) Transport move by road from St MOMELIN to St JAN-TER-BIEZEN. 1 O R admitted to Hospital	Gower Lt
BROWN CAMP	9th		Camp fatigues & working parties. Transport moved by road from St JAN-TER-BIEZEN to Brown CAMP. 2 O R admitted to Hospital.	C.S. Gower Lt

Army Form C. 2118.

WAR DIARY
or
INTELLIGENCE SUMMARY.
(Erase heading not required.)

Place	Date	Hour	Summary of Events and Information	Remarks and references to Appendices
Brown Camp	10th	—	Cleaning gun equipment etc.	
			1 O.R. returned from C.C.S.	
			1 O.R. proceeded to U.K. on leave	
			C.S. Gannon Kent	
Kempton Park	11th		The Company less transport march from Brown Camp to Kempton Park (Map Ref Belgium Sheet 28 N.W.2 C.15.6.20.40). Transport remains at Brown Camp.	
			2 O.R. admitted to hospital	
			C.S. Gannon Kent	
"	12th		Morning No 1 Section relieves a section of the 214th Coy M.G.C. in the Corps Reserve line at LANGEMARK.	Appendix VI
			Evening. No 3 & 4 Sections less pack guns relieve the 215th M.G. Coy in the front line of the Left Sector of the 175th Brigade front. The Company takes over the MGs in the Left Sector of the 175th Brigade	

WAR DIARY
or
INTELLIGENCE SUMMARY.

Army Form C. 2118.

Place	Date	Hour	Summary of Events and Information	Remarks and references to Appendices
KEMPTON P⁵			Front. Orders for relief attached	Appendix 2.
			5 OR admitted to Hospital	
			Capt PALLISER. J.S. returns from leave.	
			C.S.Gamon Lieut	
	13th		Quiet day in the line. Casualties NIL	H.Palmer Capt
"	14th		Quiet day in the line. Casualties NIL	H.Palmer Capt
"	15th		Quiet day in the line. 15 OR reinforcement arrived from Base Depôt. Casualties NIL	H.Palmer Capt

Army Form C. 2118.

WAR DIARY
or
INTELLIGENCE SUMMARY.
(Erase heading not required.)

Instructions regarding War Diaries and Intelligence Summaries are contained in F. S. Regs., Part II. and the Staff Manual respectively. Title pages will be prepared in manuscript.

Place	Date	Hour	Summary of Events and Information	Remarks and references to Appendices
KEMPTON Rd	/6		Quiet day in the line.	
"			1 OR wounded — remaining at duty.	
			Our gunners fired three rounds by Lewis on machine gun at RECQUETTE FARM.	
			2/Lieut retired from line guns. Quiet relief. Relief complete 7 p.m.	
			1 OR proceeded to U.K. on leave. J. Palmer Capt.	
"	17th		Quiet day in line. Casualties NIL. J. Palmer Capt.	
"	18th		Quiet day in line. Casualties NIL. 1 OR admitted to hospital. J. Palmer Capt.	

Army Form C. 2118.

WAR DIARY
or
INTELLIGENCE SUMMARY.

(Erase heading not required.)

Place	Date	Hour	Summary of Events and Information	Remarks and references to Appendices
KEMPTON E	19th		Quiet day in the line. Casualties Nil.	
			1 O.R. admitted to hospital. 1 O.R. rejoined from hospital. 1 Officer + 1 O.R. returned from course.	
"	20th		Quiet day in the line. Company relieved in the line by 21st M.G. Coy. Company withdrawn to CANAL BANK in reserve on relief complete. Casualties Nil.	Appendix 3
CANAL BANK	21st		Guns equipment etc cleaned. Dug-out accomodation improved. 2 Sections bathed at Divisional Baths, CANAL BANK.	

Army Form C. 2118.

WAR DIARY
or
INTELLIGENCE SUMMARY.
(Erase heading not required.)

Instructions regarding War Diaries and Intelligence Summaries are contained in F. S. Regs., Part II. and the Staff Manual respectively. Title pages will be prepared in manuscript.

Place	Date	Hour	Summary of Events and Information	Remarks and references to Appendices
SOLFERINO CAMP	22nd		Company less Transport marched from CANAL BANK to SOLFERINO CAMP.	
			Transport moved from BROWN CAMP to SOLFERINO CAMP.	
			Improving camp accommodation, have standings etc. 3 OR admitted to hospital. 1 officer and 3 OR proceed to UK on leave. J Palmer C/M	
"	23rd	7.30 a.m	Company parade under C.S.M. Clean fatigue	
		9 a.m – 12.30 p.m.	Section parades. Inspection Full marching order & personal kit. Cleaning of gun equipment and limbers. 1 OR rejoined from hospital. J Palmer O/C	

Army Form C. 2118.

WAR DIARY
or
INTELLIGENCE SUMMARY.
(Erase heading not required.)

Instructions regarding War Diaries and Intelligence Summaries are contained in F.S. Regs., Part II. and the Staff Manual respectively. Title pages will be prepared in manuscript.

Place	Date	Hour	Summary of Events and Information	Remarks and references to Appendices
SOLFERINO CAMP.	24th	7.30am	Company parade under C.S.M.	
		9 a.m	Company Parade. Drill Order.	
			1 OR reinforcement arrived from Advi Horse Transport Dept.	
			1 OR rejoined from hospital.	J Palmer Capt
"	25th	10am	Company parade for Church Parade. C. of E.	
		11.30am	R. Catholics - Mass - at St. David's Chapel - CANAL BANK. Voluntary.	
			1 OR admitted to hospital. 1 OR rejoined from hospital.	
			1 OR proceeded to U.K. on leave.	J Palmer Capt
"	26th	9am	Section parades for 1 + 2 Sections.	
		10.15am		
		9-11.30am	Section parades for 3 + 4 Sections	J Palmer Capt

Army Form C. 2118.

WAR DIARY
or
INTELLIGENCE SUMMARY.
(Erase heading not required.)

Place	Date	Hour	Summary of Events and Information	Remarks and references to Appendices
SOLFERINO CAMP	26 (cont)	10.30 a.m.	No's 1 + 2 Sections parade for Baths.	
		12.30 p.m.	No's 3 + 4 Sections parade for Baths.	
		1.30 p.m.	Transport parade for Baths.	
			1 O.R. admitted to hospital. 1 O.R. rejoined from hospital.	
			1 O.R. proceeded to U.K. on leave.	
				J. Palmer Capt.
"	27/7	9 a.m.	Company parade under C.S.M.	
		9 a.m.	Company parade. Drill order.	
		9.15 to 12.30 p.m.	Sections parades.	
			4 O.R. admitted to hospital.	
			1 O.R. proceeded to U.K. on leave.	
				J. Palmer Capt.
SOLFERINO CAMP	28th		Company less transport, moved by light Railway from SOLFERINO CAMP to KEMPTON PARK.	

Army Form C. 2118.

WAR DIARY
or
INTELLIGENCE SUMMARY.
(Erase heading not required.)

Place	Date	Hour	Summary of Events and Information	Remarks and references to Appendices
SOLFERINO CAMP	28th (cont)		No 2 & 4 sections and a sub-section of No 3 relieved 2/4 M.G. Coy in the line. Quiet relief. Relief complete 11 p.m. 1 O.R. proceeded to U.K. on leave. Casualties NIL.	
KEMPTON PARK	29th		Quiet day in the line. 1 O.R. admitted to hospital. 1 O.R. proceeded to U.K. on leave. Casualties NIL	
"	30th	8 p.m.	5 guns of the company, acting in conjunction with 1/4 Lancers of division on the left, fired 12,000 rounds on enemy strong points.	
		9 p.m.	1 O.R. proceeded to U.K. on leave.	

Army Form C. 2118.

WAR DIARY
or
INTELLIGENCE SUMMARY.
(Erase heading not required.)

Instructions regarding War Diaries and Intelligence Summaries are contained in F. S. Regs., Part II. and the Staff Manual respectively. Title pages will be prepared in manuscript.

Place	Date	Hour	Summary of Events and Information	Remarks and references to Appendices
	30th (cont)		Casualties NIL

Matthews Capt | |
| | 3/5 | | Quiet day in the line. Severe frost still holds. 4 OR reinforcements arrived from Base Depot. 2 OR admitted to hospital. 1 OR proceeded to UK on leave.

Matthews Capt. | |

Appendix 1.

198 Machine Gun Company
Move Orders No 4
6/12/17.

1. MOVE.
The Company less Transport and Advance Parties will move as follows:—
7th From Watterdal to Appanques march.
8th Appanques to Derby Bucket Camp by train.

2. ADVANCE PARTIES
(A) 4 NCO's – 60 OR's proceed to Forward area on 5th inst.
(B) 1 Officer – 30 OR's proceed to Appanques on the morning of the 6th inst.
1 Officer – 30 OR's to Derby Bucket Camp on morning of 7th inst.

3. Parades.
Company will parade on 7th inst at 9.30 AM ready to move off from Watterdal.
The Company will parade less the 2 Limbers Personnel Team on the 8th inst ready to move off at 3.15 A.M.
The 2 Limbers Personnel Team will parade on the 8th inst ready to move off at 4.45 A.M.

4. Dress.
Details of Dress will be issued later.

5. Transport.
Transport will move under orders of Transport Officer.

C. S. Gamon Lieut
for CAPTAIN,
O.C. 198th M. G. COY.

War Diary.   Appendix 2.   Copy No 9.

Relief Order No 1.
By Lieut L S Gammon
for O C 198th M G Coy
11th December 1917

Ref. SCHAAP – BALIE   1 – 10,000
      BOOEMBEEK.   1 – 10,000

1. <u>Relief</u> No 198th M.G.C will relieve part of No 215th M.G.C. and part of No 214th MGC in the left sector of the Brigade front on the 12th inst & night 12/13th Dec! 1917.

2. <u>Parades</u> No 1 Section will parade on the road ready to move at 9.30 am. This Section will relieve the Section of 214th MGC in the reserve line at LANGEMARK and EAGLE TRENCH U 24 C 2.9.
Nos 3 & 4. Sections will parade at 1.30 pm. These Sections will relieve 215th MGC in the line, No 3 relieving the left 4 guns, No 4 Section the right 2 guns. No 4 Section will only take up 2 guns for the present. Relief will take place at dusk.

3. <u>Route.</u> As shown by guide

4. <u>Equipment</u> No 1 Section will take up 4 guns 2 tripods, 44 belt boxes & accessories and will take over 2 tripods and 21 belt boxes from 214th MG Coy.
No 3 & 4 Sections will take up guns and accessories, but will take over from 215th MG Coy tripods & S A A

5. <u>Guides</u> Guides will be arranged by O C 214 & 215 MG Coys. In addition each Section will take up two men who will immediately

return to Coy HQ as guides up to sections when required.

6. <u>Rations</u>   Sections going into the line will take with them 48 hrs rations & water.

7. <u>Report</u>   OC. Sections will report "Relief Complete" by quickest route to Coy HQ at KEMPTON PARK on completion of relief.

8. <u>Returns</u>   Lists of stores taken over will be sent to Coy HQ as soon as possible. Daily Casualty Returns and Intelligence reports will be sent in daily to reach Coy HQ as early as possible each day.

Sgd C S Gammon
for O.C. 198 M.G. Coy

Copy No 1 to OC Coy
    2 to OC. No 1 Section
    3 "   "   2   "
    4 "   "   3   "
    5 "   "   4   "
    6 "   175th Inf Bde
    7 "   214th M G Coy
    8 "   215th   "   "
    9 "   War Diary
   10 "   File
   11 "   DMGO
   12 "   174th Infty Bde

Appendix 3. Relief Order of
198 M.G Company.   No 5

Ref maps - Scharp Balie.
            Blaunhoek.

1. 198 M.G Company will be relieved
on the left Divisional Sector by 214th M.G
Company on the night 20/21 Decr 1917.

2. Guides
1 Guide per Gun team will proceed
to N.B. Reserve Section. at 29th A.C.90
at dawn on the 20/12/17 and will
await arrival of relieving teams.
Reserve Guns will relieve by day.
Gun teams to keep at least 200 yards
interval along the duck boards.
     Gun teams of forward positions
will not leave reserve section HQ.
before 3.15 P.M.

3. Tripods & Belt Boxes will be handed
over to 214 M.G. Company on relief.
All other material including empty
Petrol Tins will be carried back
to Reserve section HQ where these
stores will be loaded on a limber.

4. Section Officers will ensure that
all information is handed over to
incoming Gun teams by Gun team
Commanders.

5. Receipts for Belt Boxes and Tripods
will be handed in to Company
Office.

6. Section Officers will detail 1 N.C.O. to remain at each position till morning. Gun teams are satisfied they know their line of fire and are acquainted with standing orders.

7. On relief Lt Donovan will load his material into a Limber at his H.Q. and will detail a Guard of 1 NCO & 2 men to remain with this Limber & see that all material is loaded up. Limber will not leave till every Gun team has passed.

8. Gun teams will proceed independently to H.A Bridge where Guides will take them to quarters at Canal Bank. Limber will also return to H.A Bridge where Guide will meet it.

Acknowledge.

Issued at 9 A.M. 19/12/17

Copy No 1. Lt Donovan
       2.   Lt Reid
       3.   Lt Grant
       4.   214 M.G. Coy
       5.   War Diary
       6.   File

J.D. Talbot
CAPTAIN,
O.C. 198th M. G. COY.

CONFIDENTIAL

WAR DIARY

of

198th Company

Machine Gun Corps

from ~~December~~ January 1st 1918
to February 1st 1918

Volume XIV (Original)

Army Form C. 2118.

WAR DIARY
or
INTELLIGENCE SUMMARY.
(Erase heading not required.)

Instructions regarding War Diaries and Intelligence Summaries are contained in F. S. Regs., Part II. and the Staff Manual respectively. Title pages will be prepared in manuscript.

Place	Date	Hour	Summary of Events and Information	Remarks and references to Appendices
KEMPTON PARK	1918 JAN 1		No 1 Section and a Subsection of No 3 relieved No 4 Section & Subsection of No 3 in the line – Quiet Relief – Relief complete at 8 P.M. (Arnachio Other Ranks 1 (slightly wounded) 2 O.R. proceeded to U.K. on leave	
"	2		Quiet day in the line. 1 O.R. joins from Base. 1 O.R. rejoins Unit from C.C.S. 1 O.R. proceeded on leave to U.K.	
"	3		Quiet day in the line – apart from direct hit on Senegal 4th man removed his H.Q. to Laube. 1 O.R. joins from Base 1 O.R. proceeded on leave to U.K.	

Army Form C. 2118.

WAR DIARY
or
INTELLIGENCE SUMMARY.
(Erase heading not required.)

Instructions regarding War Diaries and Intelligence Summaries are contained in F. S. Regs., Part II, and the Staff Manual respectively. Title pages will be prepared in manuscript.

Place	Date	Hour	Summary of Events and Information	Remarks and references to Appendices
KEMPTON PARK	1918 Jan 4		Re/Recon Subsection of No 3 Section relieved in bivouac nr Cuss by 2th M.G. Coy and Company repairs Bivouacs at Solferino Camp. Roster camp heavily shelled during early morning. 1 O.R. wounded (remained at duty)	
SOLFERINO CAMP	5		Company engaged all day cleaning bivouacs and packing up preparatory to move to TUNNELLING CAMP.	
do	6	9 A.M.	Company paraded for Tuchweering Order mapping. Remainder of day engaged in preparation for move	
do	7	7.30 A.M.	Company less Transport proceed to TUNNELLING CAMP by Rail via ELVERDINGHE. Transport proceed by road. At Army 3 O.R. proceed on leave at CASSIERS. 3 O.R. proceed on leave to U.K.	

Army Form C. 2118.

WAR DIARY
or
INTELLIGENCE SUMMARY.
(Erase heading not required.)

Place	Date	Hour	Summary of Events and Information	Remarks and references to Appendices
TONNELLING CAMP	1918 Jan 8	10 A.M.	Company and Transport paraded by Road and were sent Camp - ROAD CAMP - after unpacking blanketels 2 O.R.³ proceed on leave to U.K.	
ROAD CAMP	9	7.30 A.M.	Company paraded under C.S.M. (P.T. and Running.)	
		9 A.M.	Company paraded for Inspection - Drill Order - numerous of morning under Section arrangements - Equipmentsfaus, Kit Inspection.	
			1 Officer & 10 O.R. return from leave	
	10	7.20	Company parade under C.S.M. (P.T. and Running)	
		9 A.M.	Company Parade - Drill Order - Squad drill - saluting &c.	
		10 A.M.	Company Parade - P.T. - running drill	
		11 to 1 p.m.	Gun drill & stoppages, mechanism etc.	

Army Form C. 2118.

WAR DIARY
or
INTELLIGENCE SUMMARY.
(Erase heading not required.)

Instructions regarding War Diaries and Intelligence
Summaries are contained in F. S. Regs., Part II.
and the Staff Manual respectively. Title pages
will be prepared in manuscript.

Place	Date	Hour	Summary of Events and Information	Remarks and references to Appendices
Road Camp	1918 Nov 11	7.30 a 9 am 10 a 11 am 1 pm	Company parade under C.S.M. Company parade P.T. running drill Gun drill S.A. D.TC Cleaning of machine gun Equipment, and chit-lectore-entyre-discipline.	
	12		Sunday.- Church Parade.	
	13	7.30 9. 10. 11. 3pm	C.S.M. Parade Squad drill - discipline P.C. Gas drill & inspection of gas appliances Remainder of morning gun drill, IA, mechanism P/C Company had baths.	
	14	7.30 9.	C.S.M. Lectures under Section Officers for P.T and running drill followed by machine gun work, stripping IA P/C	

D. D. & L., London, E.C.
(A8004) Wt W1771/M2931 750,000 5/17 Sch. 52 Forms/C2118/14

Army Form C. 2118.

WAR DIARY
or
INTELLIGENCE SUMMARY.

(Erase heading not required.)

Instructions regarding War Diaries and Intelligence Summaries are contained in F. S. Regs., Part II. and the Staff Manual respectively. Title pages will be prepared in manuscript.

Place	Date	Hour	Summary of Events and Information	Remarks and references to Appendices
ROAD CAMP.	1918 Jan 15	9am	Company parade for inspection - full marching order.	
		9.30-11	Running drill & P.T.	
		11am-1pm	Overhauling & cleaning all gun materials & spare parts	
	16	7.30	C.O.m.s Parade	
		9am	Rate march, once - Full Marching order.	
	17	7.30	C.O.m.s Parade	
		9	Squad drill, deckline &c	
		10.	P.T. & Running drill	
		11.30-1pm	Gun drill. I.A. mechanism &c	
	18	7.30.	C.O.m.s Parade	
		9am	Section parades, limbers, guns, gun equipment & ammunition	
		4pm	Cleaned and reported prompt to move. All officers attended a lecture by the G.O.C. 5.2nd Division at the Church Army Hut. TUNNELLING CAMP. Subject: The principles of defence	

WAR DIARY
or
INTELLIGENCE SUMMARY.
(Erase heading not required.)

Army Form C. 2118.

Place	Date	Hour	Summary of Events and Information	Remarks and references to Appendices
ROAD CAMP	1918 Jan 19	8.45a 5.pm	Company parade under C.S.M for general fatigues. Company paraded at 5-pm and proceed by road to PROVEN. The Transport joined the Column at the Transport lines. Mt Gamn acted as T.O. during the move. Breakfast rations for the 20 were carried on the man, the remainder in bulk in G.S. wagon. The entraining was carried out without a hitch. Time of departure from PROVEN. - 10.30 p.m.	
	20		Detrained at VILLERS BRETONNEUX at 2 pm, and after unloading Transport, proceeded by road to COURCELLES, and took over billets.	Appendix I
COURCELLES	21	9	General fatigues under O.S.M. cleaning up billets, and cleaning limbers after move.	
	22	7 9.30 10 12-	C.S.M.S Parade NCOs under C.S.M. Lectures P.T. Gun drill, stripping etc Gun drill, saluting etc	

Army Form C. 2118.

WAR DIARY
or
INTELLIGENCE SUMMARY.
(Erase heading not required.)

Instructions regarding War Diaries and Intelligence Summaries are contained in F. S. Regs., Part II. and the Staff Manual respectively. Title pages will be prepared in manuscript.

Place	Date	Hour	Summary of Events and Information	Remarks and references to Appendices
COURCELLES	1916. Jan 23	9	Company parade for Rate March. Drill Order. Route: COURCELLES. MARCELCAVE - VILLERS-BRETONNEUX - Billets	
	24	7.30	C.2.m.s. Parade	
		9-11	No 1 & 2 Sections firing on range. Stoppages Etc. No 3 & 4 do. ½ hr PT + Running drill ½ hr Another practise without firing ½ hr Saluting. Squad drill Etc.	
		11-1	1 hr Section change round. 2 nd Lieut W F PURSER is taken on the strength of the unit with effect from 22-1-18. and is posted to No 1 Section as 2nd Section Officer.	
	25	7.30.	C.S.M.s Parade	
		9am	Sections PT + Running drill	
		10 -	Gas Inspection + Gas drill	
		11am-1pm	Pack saddlery, Movement across country Etc	

Army Form C. 2118.

WAR DIARY
or
INTELLIGENCE SUMMARY.
(Erase heading not required.)

Instructions regarding War Diaries and Intelligence Summaries are contained in F. S. Regs., Part II. and the Staff Manual respectively. Title pages will be prepared in manuscript.

Place	Date	Hour	Summary of Events and Information	Remarks and references to Appendices
COURCELLES	1918 26	9am	Brigade Route March in drill order.	
	27.	10.15a	Church Parade C of E under Orderly Officer. Roll Call P.M. Helmsmann. SOC	
			Afternoon Inspection of Anti-Gas appliances	
			Capt Hitchcock is taken on strength from 26-1-18.	
	28.	7.30a	C.E.M. Parade	
		9am.	No 1 & 2 Sections firing on 400yds range.	
			" 3. 4 do NCOs lecture CSM. Lectures PT & running	
		10am- 11.0p	Infantry drill	
			Packsaddlery.	
	29.	7am	C.E.M. Parade	
		9a.	Sections under Section Officers PT & Running, NCOs lecture CSM Squad drill.	
		10am to	Gun drill, belt filling, stripping.	
		12.30p 12.30 to 1p.	Lecture - subject discipline	

WAR DIARY
or
INTELLIGENCE SUMMARY.

Army Form C. 2118.

Place	Date	Hour	Summary of Events and Information	Remarks and references to Appendices
COURCELLES	1918 June 30.	7am	B.M.A Parade	
		9	Sections PT & Running. NCOs under OSM. Squad drill Dto	
		10	Gas Dto with guns.	
		11am to 1pm	Open order drill with guns	
	31	9am	Lectures firing and stoppages on 400yds range.	
		9am	do PT and Running	
		10a	do Infantry drill	
		11-1pm	do Gas drill Dto	

Appendix I

198 Machine Gun Company.

O.C. Company.
Copy 8

Move Order.

Secret.

I. 58th Division will be transferred to 3rd Corps Fifth Army on the 19th inst.

II. 198th Machine Gun Company will move with 174th Inf Bde. group on the 19th inst, entraining on No 5 Train, Serial No 26.
   Time of Departure — 9.30 pm
   Probable time of arrival 9.30 am. 20th inst.
   Entraining Station — PROVEN.
   Detraining Station — VILLERS-BRETONNEUX.

III. Company will parade in Camp at 5 pm and proceed by road to PROVEN. The Transport will join the Column at the Transport lines and will be ready to move off at 5.15 pm. Lt Gamon will act as T.O. during the move. Transport will carry nosebags & hay nets filled. Breastropes & 14 water buckets will be carried on water cart.

IV. Breakfast rations for the 20th inst will be carried on the man. Remainder of Rations will travel in bulk on the G.S. wagon. Waterbottles will be filled by 12 noon on the 19th inst. This water must not be touched before the Company has entrained. One blanket per man will be carried. Second blankets will be carried in Section limbers. On no account must personal kit be carried in limbers.

V. Entraining

A. 2/Lt Smith will report to Capt Crofts 2/6th Bn. Brigade Entraining Officer at PROVEN at 5.45 pm. on the 19th inst and report the arrival of the Company at 6.15 pm. He will also hand over the Entraining State in triplicate to the Officers clerk (Rfm Goddard) at R.T.O.s office as soon as he arrives.

B. Transport will be drawn up on the platform from North end into Double Column, vehicles being kept together opposite the flats. Animals will then be unhooked and led away to water. On returning from watering, animals will be lined up opposite Trucks allotted to them, and men and animals equipment will be stacked on side of platform away from the train.
The Company will take off equipment

C. CSM will detail parties as under:-

1. 1 L/Cpl + 2 men to fill water troughs on Station
2. 1 NCO + 6 men to report to B.T.O with breastropes for horse trucks. These will be carried on water cart.
3. 1 NCO + 6 men to fill petrol cans for horse trucks
4. Sufficient brakesmen to allow each driver one man to take his harness. These men will report to Transport lines after dinner on the 19th inst.
5. 6 men to help the grooms with Saddlery to report with brakesmen.
6. 1 NCO + 2 men as guard over mens equipment
7. 1 NCO + 2 men to collect pole bars and load on HQ Truck.
8. CSM will fall in remainder of the Company and report to Lt Jaurie

D. Lt Jaurie with 2/Lt Trent will be in charge of party (8) who will act as entraining party under orders of Bde Entraining Officer.

E. 2/Lt Donovan will be in charge of Parties 1, 2, 3, 6 & 7 and will superintend these duties. Breast ropes, water buckets and petrol cans for Parties (2) and (3) will be loaded on the water cart. Petrol cans and water buckets will not be loaded until animals are entrained

F. Transport Officer will make arrangements for tea to be made for Transport at PROVEN station. 2 biscuits per section and one for HQ will be carried in the trucks. Party (7) will be responsible for drawing these from the ~~Cooks~~ cart. Tea will be made at ABBEVILLE (where hot water is available) under Section arrangements.

G. Party (3) will fill 28 petrol cans and when animals are entrained, they will put 4 cans of water and 2 water buckets in each horse wagon. They will report to 2/Lt Donovan when this is completed.

H. No man is allowed to leave PROVEN, or ABBEVILLE stations without permission from an Officer.

VI. No man must leave the train without permission of an Officer. The Senior NCO in the truck will be held responsible that this order is obeyed.

Detraining
   Ref Para V
  (a) Party (1) will join party (8)
  (b) Party (2) will help drivers and recover breastropes
  (c) Party (3) will collect petrol cans and waterbuckets and load on water cart.
  (d) Party (4) will take charge of drivers harness and equipment, which will be dumped well away from the train.
  (e) Party (6) perform same duties.
  (f) Party (7) replace pole bars when limbers are unloaded.
  (g) C.S.M will fall in remainder of Company, dump kits and report to Lt Laurie
  (h) Lt Laurie will be in charge of detraining party, and will be under orders of Bde detraining officer Lt Mills

(i) 2/Lt Donovan will report when his parties have completed their respective duties.

(j) The Senior NCO in each truck will be held responsible that nothing is left in the truck after detraining

VII T.O. and Section Officers will explain to their men any portion of these orders that concern them.

C.S.M will ensure that N.C.O's detailed understand their separate duties

Issued 6pm.
17.1.18.

[signature]
CAPTAIN,
O.C. 198th M. G. Coy.

Copies to O.C Company 8
Lt. Gamon 5
Lt. Laurie 3
2/Lt. Donovan 4
2/Lt. Smith 1
2/Lt. Trent 2
C.S.M. Cox 6
a/2nd. Jones. 7
War diary 8

SECRET

98th Machine Gun Coy

WAR DAIRY

VOLUME XV

FEB 1918

Army Form C. 2118.

WAR DIARY
or
INTELLIGENCE SUMMARY.
(Erase heading not required.)

Instructions regarding War Diaries and Intelligence Summaries are contained in F. S. Regs., Part II. and the Staff Manual respectively. Title pages will be prepared in manuscript.

Place	Date	Hour	Summary of Events and Information	Remarks and references to Appendices
COURCELLES	1918 2nd	9 P.M.	Company (less Transport) Parade full marching order for Route March – Marched 10 miles approx. Bivouaced [signature] CAPTAIN, O.C. 103th M.G. Coy.	
do	2nd	7 A.M.	C.S.M's Parade	
		9-11 A.M.	No 30th Rechin Firing and Stoppages at 400 yds range	
		9-10 A.M.	No 2 Rechin P.T. and Running	
		10-11 A.M.	do Musketry &c	
		11-1 P.M.	do Infantry Drill &c [signature] CAPTAIN, O.C. 103th M.G. Coy.	
do	3rd	9 A.M.	Church Parade for Roman Catholics	
		11 A.M.	do Church of England [signature] CAPTAIN, O.C. 103th M.G. Coy.	
do	4th	7 A.M.	C.S.M's Parade	
		9 A.M.	" Rechin Pt. Running – N.C.O's Parade under C.S.M.	
		10-11 A.M.	Gas drill – No 2 Rechin Grenade throwing	
		11-12	Gun drill etc – No 3 Rechin practice Grenade throwing	
		12-1 P.M.	No 1 Rechin Grenade throwing – Men doing this for 1st time inspected with grenade throwing [signature] CAPTAIN, O.C. 103th M.G. Coy.	

Army Form C. 2118.

WAR DIARY
or
INTELLIGENCE SUMMARY.
(Erase heading not required.)

Instructions regarding War Diaries and Intelligence Summaries are contained in F. S. Regs., Part II. and the Staff Manual respectively. Title pages will be prepared in manuscript.

Place	Date	Hour	Summary of Events and Information	Remarks and references to Appendices
COURCELLES	19.18 5th	7 AM.	CSM's Parade	
		9-10AM.	P.T. and Running Drill	
		10-11AM.	No 1 Action - General Theory	
			Gun Drill - No 2 Section - Grenade Theory	
		11-12 Noon	Lecture Gas Drill - No 3 Section - Revision	
			No 3 Section Grenade Theory	
		12-1 PM.	Sections to have went round through Grenade Theory	
			No 1 Section Grenade Theory	
		6 to 8 PM.	No 1 & 2 Sections Parade for firing live Grenades	
		10-11AM.	P.T. Running - Gunfire drill	
		5 AM.	No 3rd Section P.T. Running. Gunfire drill	
		10-11AM.	No 3rd section - Revision - Throwing live Grenades	
	7th 7AM.	Transport and Athletic Parade under OS Gunner Musketry Rope	
			Company Parade under CSM.	
		9AM.	Gas Training with Guns	

Signatures: O.C. 198th M.G. Coy. CAPTAIN
O.C. 198th M.G. Coy. CAPTAIN

Army Form C. 2118.

WAR DIARY
or
INTELLIGENCE SUMMARY.
(Erase heading not required.)

Instructions regarding War Diaries and Intelligence Summaries are contained in F. S. Regs., Part II. and the Staff Manual respectively. Title pages will be prepared in manuscript.

Place	Date	Hour	Summary of Events and Information	Remarks and references to Appendices
COURCELLES	1918 7th April	10 AM	L.T. Murray-Phipps	
		11 AM	returning from 6 spare parts	
		12-1 PM	Company Parade	
				Walker CAPTAIN O.C. 199th M.G. Coy.
ROYE	8	7-30 AM	Transport proceed by road to CRISSOLLES.	
COURCELLES		7 AM	Company Parade. Proceed by road to VILLERS BRETTONEUX - thence by train to APILLY - then by Buses to MARIZEELE.	
				Walker CAPTAIN O.C. 199th M.G. Coy.
CRISSOLLES	9	7 AM	Transport proceed by road to MARIZEELE rejoining Company Company take over in line from 90 Machine Gun Coy. relief 16 guns in the line	
				Walker CAPTAIN O.C. 199th M.G. Coy.
MARIZEELE	10	8 AM to 12-30 PM	Details engaged in Camp fatigue - Billet area fatigue, cleaning ammunition Company in line - No Casualties - Line Quiet	
				Walker CAPTAIN O.C. 199th M.G. Coy.
do	11	8 AM to 4 PM	Details engaged all day as above. Line quiet - no casualties -	
				Walker CAPTAIN O.C. 199th M.G. Coy.

WAR DIARY
or
INTELLIGENCE SUMMARY.
(Erase heading not required.)

Army Form C. 2118.

Place	Date	Hour	Summary of Events and Information	Remarks and references to Appendices
MARICELF	1918 Apr 12	8 AM to 4 PM	Details engaged all day in billet area fatigues etc Company in line - nothing to report. No casualties [signed] CAPTAIN, O.C. 198th M.G. Coy	
do	13	8 AM to 4 PM	Details engaged all day as ahead. Company in line - no casualties - [signed] CAPTAIN, O.C. 198th M.G. Coy	
do	14	8 AM to 4 PM	Details engaged all day as above. No casualties in the line - very quiet.	
		12 NN	55373 Acting Corp Hartley F.A. tried by F.G.C.M. Finding to be investigated later. [signed] CAPTAIN, O.C. 198th M.G. Coy	
do	15	8 AM to 4 PM	Details engaged all day as ahead. Company in line - no casualties - [signed] CAPTAIN, O.C. 198th M.G. Coy	
do	16	8 AM to 4 PM	Details engaged all day in making shells etc burnt punt - air raid - 2 aeroplanes dropped 10 bombs greater part N.E. of Maricelf. Company in line - no casualties [signed] CAPTAIN, O.C. 198th M.G. Coy	

Army Form C. 2118.

WAR DIARY
or
INTELLIGENCE SUMMARY.
(Erase heading not required.)

Instructions regarding War Diaries and Intelligence Summaries are contained in F. S. Regs., Part II. and the Staff Manual respectively. Title pages will be prepared in manuscript.

Place	Date	Hour	Summary of Events and Information	Remarks and references to Appendices
MARIZEELE	1918 Sep 17	8 AM to 4 PM	Details engaged all day in making clothing bulletproof - 3 E.A. appeared H.N.E. of Mangerre at 6.50 PM dropping 34 shots - and landed 12 above. Company in line - Casualties nil	J. Walker CAPTAIN O.C. 198th M.G. Coy.
do	18	8 AM to 4 PM	Details engaged as above and on general camp fatigues all day. Company in line - Casualties nil	J. Walker CAPTAIN O.C. 198th M.G. Coy.
do	19	8 AM to 4 PM	Details engaged all day - on clothing, billet area and company fatigues - No casualties. Company in line.	J. Walker CAPTAIN O.C. 198th M.G. Coy.
do	20	8 AM to 4 PM	Details engaged all day on above. Company in line - No casualties	J. Walker CAPTAIN O.C. 198th M.G. Coy.
do	21	8 AM to 4 PM	Details engaged all day as above. Company in line - No casualties	J. Walker CAPTAIN O.C. 198th M.G. Coy.

Army Form C. 2118.

WAR DIARY
or
INTELLIGENCE SUMMARY.
(Erase heading not required.)

Instructions regarding War Diaries and Intelligence
Summaries are contained in F. S. Regs., Part II.
and the Staff Manual respectively. Title pages
will be prepared in manuscript.

Place	Date	Hour	Summary of Events and Information	Remarks and references to Appendices
MM IZEELE	1918 Feb 22	8 A.M. to 4 P.M.	Details engaged all day in Miller Ridge - Entrenching, revetting traverses - no casualties. Company in line.	[signed] CAPTAIN, O.C. 198th M. G. Coy.
	23	8 A.M. to 4 P.M.	Details engaged all day as above. Company in line - no casualties.	[signed] CAPTAIN, O.C. 198th M. G. Coy.
	24	8 A.M. to 4 P.M.	Details engaged all day as above. Company in line - 1 other rank (H) th Batt'n London Regiment slightly wounded - remained at duty	[signed] CAPTAIN, O.C. 198th M. G. Coy.
	25	9 A.M. to 4 P.M.	Details engaged all day as above. Company in line - no casualties.	[signed] CAPTAIN, O.C. 198th M. G. Coy.
	26	8 A.M. to 4 P.M.	Details engaged all day as above. Company in line - no casualties.	[signed] CAPTAIN, O.C. 198th M. G. Coy.
	27	8 A.M. to 4 P.M.	Details engaged all day as above. Company in Rear - Locrehof	[signed] CAPTAIN, O.C. 198th M. G. Coy.
	28	8 A.M. to 4 P.M.	Details engaged all day as above. Company in rear - no casualties	[signed] CAPTAIN, O.C. 198th M. G. Coy.

www.ingramcontent.com/pod-product-compliance
Lightning Source LLC
Chambersburg PA
CBHW081409160426
43193CB00013B/2143